PENGUIN BOOKS
SPOUSE

Shobhaa Dé describes herself as an 'obsessive-compulsive writer.'
Columnist, commentator, and author of fourteen books, she
lives with her family in Mumbai, a city that she considers a
'character', not just a locale, in her work.

She is currently planning her next book, a novel.

Spouse

The Truth About Marriage

SHOBHAA DE'

PENGUIN BOOKS

PENGUIN BOOKS

Published by the Penguin Group

Penguin Books India Pvt. Ltd, 11 Community Centre, Panchsheel Park, New Delhi 110 017, India

Penguin Group (USA) Inc., 375 Hudson Street, New York, New York 10014, USA

Penguin Group (Canada), 10 Alcorn Avenue, Toronto, Ontario, Canada M4V 3B2 (a division of Pearson Penguin Canada Inc.)

Penguin Books Ltd, 80 Strand, London WC2R 0RL, England

Penguin Ireland, 25 St. Stephen's Green, Dublin 2, Ireland (a division of Penguin Books Ltd)

Penguin Group (Australia), 250 Camberwell Road, Camberwell, Victoria 3124, Australia (a division of Pearson Australia Group Pty Ltd)

Penguin Group (NZ), cnr Airborne and Rosedale Roads, Albany, Auckland 1310, New Zealand (a division of Pearson New Zealand Ltd)

Penguin Group (South Africa) (Pty) Ltd, 24 Sturdee Avenue, Rosebank, Johannesburg 2196, South Africa

Penguin Books Ltd, Registered Offices: 80 Strand, London WC2R 0RL, England

First published by Penguin Books India 2005

Copyright © Shobhaa Dé 2005

The quote on page 283 is from *Hindu Samskaras: Socio-religious Study of the Hindu Sacraments* (p. 228) by Rajbali Pandey, published by Motilal Banarasidass, 2002.

Typeset in Perpetua by Mantra Virtual Services, New Delhi

Printed at Chaman Offset Printers, New Delhi

For all spouses
For mine
For Dilip

Contents

Introduction

There's no such thing as a 'perfect marriage' or a 'perfect spouse'. Come on, get real! Marriage is a flawed institution, if you buy into that theory. Nor is it—as diehard romantics would have you think—a sublime, divine and idyllic union, a true meeting of two bodies, minds and souls.

Marriage is an idea. A malleable idea. Marriage is what you make of it. Marriage is maddening, as anybody who has experienced it will tell you. There is no formula for a happy marriage. And nobody has all the answers.

When two people take the plunge, they do so with the hope that their marriage will last for ever and ever. Often, it doesn't. Things can, and do go, horribly wrong. Why? Can anything be done to prevent a marriage from going on the rocks?

I believe the institution of marriage is under threat. Not just in India, but all over the world. 'Who needs it?' I'm frequently challenged. It is this question that served as a trigger for this book. Why are people turning away from an institution that has survived for centuries? The only social contract that has worked across cultures? Why has the C-word (commitment) disappeared from relationships? What are we afraid of? Why is modern marriage struggling for survival? Is 'love' the single most terrifying word in our dictionary today? Why does permanence scare us? Have we forgotten what it means to give ourselves unconditionally to a life-partner? Do we even want to?

Marriage overwhelms people. Especially young people. Why should it? Too many questions. Too few answers . . .

Marriage is memory. If the good memories outnumber the bad ones, it's fair to declare the marriage a success. Marriage is also about moments. It depends entirely on which ones are cherished. Anybody who is married, or has ever been married, will recognize the truth of this deceptively simple sentence: marriage is for those who believe in it, who actively want it, who enjoy it.

This is exactly what I told my twenty-eight-year-old son as we drove back from my fourteen-year-old daughter's school. He was leaving on a short business trip. I got the feeling he was meeting an old girlfriend in London.

I was keen to ask, but thought better of it, reasoning to myself that had he wanted to share that little piece of information with me in the first place, he'd have mentioned it himself. However, I was concerned. Much as I liked his ex, I also knew she wasn't 'the one'. Besides, she was between marriages and back in touch with all her old boyfriends. While images of the two of them in the days they were together flashed through my mind, I also sent up a private prayer. 'Oh God!' I beseeched the one above, 'please spare my son . . .'

It was as if he'd read my mind, for at that very moment, he said, 'Relax, Mother, I'm not thinking of marrying her. Actually, I'm not thinking of marriage, period.' Phew! That was close. By now, the fourteen-year-old was listening keenly. 'But why aren't you married yet? Most of your friends are . . .' she said.

My son laughed. 'I don't think I'm ready for it . . . In a way, I'm very selfish. And you can't afford to be too selfish in a marriage.'

Selfish. It's such an awful word. I tossed it around inside my head. Selfish. Self-focused. Self-centred. Self-obsessed. Self-absorbed. Self. Self. Self. That was it—the elusive word I'd been looking for. It became the key to writing this book. For it is this four-letter word—self—which eventually determines the quality of what I consider the single most difficult, challenging, exhilarating relationship in the world.

If there is too much 'self' in marriage, it doesn't work. If there's too little, well, that doesn't work either.

I have been 'watching' marriages closely—my own included. Believe me, there have been times when I've felt exasperated enough to throw up my hands and say, 'God! Who needs it?' The more I watch, the more I learn. And the answer to that question ('Who needs it?') is obvious: almost everybody I know. Even couples trapped in the most awful marriages.

If one begins to think of marriage as a basic human 'need', one then starts examining its downside a little more sympathetically. I must confess that as a committed 'watcher', I've often been baffled by aspects of marriage that defy logic itself.

My two sisters and I frequently discuss the nitty-gritties of modern marriage. We also discuss the marriage of our parents, besides each other's. At the end of our talkathons, we are frequently so drained by our dissections, we retreat into a cool space with a silly book and emerge feeling even more baffled. Any discussion on marriage is like that— vexing.

'Don't even think of getting married,' I told my second son, 'you are not cut out for it.' He nodded in agreement. Encouraged by his response, I added, 'In fact, your entire generation should skip marriage. You people have absolutely no idea what goes into a marriage. You are way too impatient and intolerant. At the first sign of trouble, you're ready to walk. Look at your friends' marriages. Not even a couple of years into the marriage and it's already over.' I felt a little sorry hearing my own words. But I knew that what I'd said was basically true. I'd seen far too many young marriages fall apart on grounds that seemed astonishingly superficial. With both partners on a shorter-than-short fuse, unwilling to meet the other halfway, is it any wonder that most of the clubs and lounge bars in Mumbai are full of desperately lonely divorced people under thirty?

'Do you have a different set of standards for your daughters?' a girlfriend asked me recently. 'Absolutely not!' I assured her. I tell the girls exactly the same thing—do not marry because you feel you must, you have to, it's the done thing. Do not marry because you want children but not necessarily marriage. Do not marry for the sake of some imaginary 'security', for none exists. Marry because you want to marry. Because you believe in it. Because you wish to share your life with someone you care about. Only then will that marriage survive and thrive.

Marriage, most people would agree, is unnatural. Two strangers with nothing in common other than a vague attraction, agree to spend their lives together. Absurd. Illogical. Dangerous. But hey, nobody has come up with a better option so far. Unless I've missed something.

Can marriage ever work according to a rule-book? Is it

possible, or even desirable, to fit marriage into convenient slots? Frankly, no. Marriage is erratic. Marriage is mad. It is also frustrating, infuriating, annoying and unpredictable. When I look back on mine and reflect on its many phases, there are times when I think I must have been crazy to have done/said/thought what I did. Then I switch gears and think about other, quieter, more mellow moments and smile to myself.

Marriage, with all its complex, complicated, dizzying ingredients remains my number one comfort zone. I guess, at the end of the day, that's all that counts. This book has forced me to turn the searchlight on my own relationships. Not just with my husband Dilip, but also my children, my father, my sisters, brother and friends. Often, I've averted my eyes, not wanting to deal with what I've seen. But more often than that, I've gasped with delight at fragmented images that have emerged—rarely intact or entirely accurate, but so what? These have filled my heart with joy and I've lingered over them and savoured the refreshed memory of those special moments.

No marriage, regardless of how 'good' it is or how 'successful', is without its blights and flaws. Mine isn't any different. There has been tumult and turbulence, conflict and rage. I've questioned, attributed, accused and insinuated. Sometimes, these outbursts have left me feeling like an absolute idiot. At other times, I've felt self-righteous and martyred. On a few occasions, I've confided my worst feelings to my children (who better to advise me? Who else can be trusted so completely?). But through all of that, I've never doubted one thing: marriage. And if I dare now to comment on the institution, I do so armed with skills and insights I would never have possessed had I opted out. The fact is, I like being married. I enjoy being recognized as a 'married lady'. Mrs so-and-so. I take pride in my marital status. And never ever feel the need to disguise, camouflage or play it down.

While this book isn't exactly a marriage manual in the usual sense of the word, what it definitely is, is a strong endorsement for being married and staying married. The idea is to think about, discuss and share the vital emotions that go into building a relationship—often with a stranger. If the materials used in this unique construction are of an inferior quality, the edifice will collapse even before getting to stage two. But if no compromise is made on the bricks and mortar used, gradually a marvellously strong structure will stand tall, each room filled with laughter, love, tears and sentiment.

I thought of all this in a fragmented way over a dim-sum lunch with my husband. It was a few days after his birthday. He insisted it was the best he'd ever celebrated. The SMS from him, asking me to lunch, came while I was in the middle of an intense and exhaustive interview with a lovely American journalist. Normally, he and I avoid 'doing lunch' (as they say these days). I like doing away with it altogether, while he prefers a quick sandwich at the club. But this was obviously special. Maybe it was his way of saying 'thank you' for organizing his birthday dinner (not that I'd slaved, but it had gone off well).

I hurriedly wrapped up the interview and rushed to meet Dé at our favourite Chinese restaurant. He was eager to talk about his response to a film he'd seen the previous evening on TV—*Unfaithful,* starring Richard Gere. I was equally eager to tell him about the film I'd seen with our daughters while he was away at the farmhouse in Alibag. I let him go first and was half-amused, half-surprised by the passion with which he spoke about the characters and their compulsions. This was comparatively new. I was the die-hard movie buff cramming my head with film trivia. Dé watched movies mechanically, preferring thrillers, gangster hits, guy films, war epics.

Unfaithful was about relationships. In fact, it fell into the category of chick-flicks on account of its central theme—why happily married women stray. Dé analyzed it from different angles and wonder of wonders, he found something sympathetic to say about the woman. I couldn't believe my ears and said so. It was turning out to be an interesting lunch. Just as we were about to pronounce a joint verdict on the Richard Gere character, a noisy lady rushed up to our table to greet us. 'I had to break it up,' she announced loudly. 'This is too much—how long have you been married?' We shared a laugh, a smart repartee and left the restaurant. The mood continued as we decided to walk to the club, which was close by. Dé took my hand and we strolled at a leisurely pace, enjoying Mumbai's brief winter and the mild February sun.

At the ice cream counter, we decided to indulge in a creamy, rich custard-apple ice cream. As always, Dé ordered one scoop with two spoons. We lingered over the gooey treat even as casual friends stopped for a few words—the same ones! 'Are you okay?' 'What's wrong with you?' 'Romantic twosome? Let's get a camera . . .' It seemed to amaze people that a husband-and-wife could take time off on a Monday afternoon just to spend a couple of hours chatting and enjoying each other's company. I felt sad at their reaction since it made a powerful statement on the state of most marriages—their own included. Has urban society become so jaded and cynical that a couple is made to feel weird for choosing to spend time with each other? Is it so uncommon as to warrant comment?

The same evening, Dé came home with a small gift. It was his way of saying he'd spent a great afternoon and that we should do it more often. At this point, I must clarify that Dé is the real romantic in this marriage. It is he who drives it, it is he who sets the pace and steers it in the direction he considers appropriate. Frankly, I'm a bit too practical, too prosaic, and left to myself, would settle for a marriage defined by comfort rather than high romance. Not that I don't enjoy these moments, I just don't actively create them. The candles and roses routine is better handled by my husband, who in his quest for the 'perfect evening' is known to go to extremes our children find most amusing.

I love the attention, welcome the hoopla. But at the same time, much as I hate to admit it, the strain of keeping up gets to me. I mean, how guilty do I feel? Here is a man who invests so much time in creating an amazing ambience for a private dinner at our farmhouse. And here I am, passively participating in an elaborate ritual, feeling cherished but also slightly detached.

Later, I read an SMS that says, 'Thanks for a wonderful day' and my heart breaks. Once again, I'm reminded of the fact that marriage is about moments. Moments like this one—poignant in its short life. Hit the 'delete' button, and it's wiped out. Linger a few extra seconds, and it becomes meaningful. How many of us bother to do that? I try. But I frequently fail. Aware as I am that these micro-seconds of connecting with one's partner during the frenzy of a crowded work day are precious, even profound, I still let them go unacknowledged. Even the mental act of saying 'Must respond' negates the moment. That's how impersonal life has become, even with those closest to you. Imagine the irony of sending memos to yourself. Imagine the tragedy of reminders to prompt you to respond to a beloved's message of love. I find it disgraceful; I promise to make amends. But even that thought makes me feel low.

Slow down, my children tell me. Chill out. Dé himself takes over and compels me to take time off . . . Relax, he advises, smoothening the furrow between my brows with a gentle massage. I can feel the tense muscles of my taut neck gradually starting to relax.

Contemporaries laugh when I talk about the importance of romance in marriage. Fine at twenty, they scoff . . . but at our age? Well, romance is a given at twenty. It is 'our age' that tosses it out of the window, demeans and reduces its value. I wonder why. Do we find it that scary? I know couples who display revulsion at the thought of romancing one another. Yes, revulsion. I've seen women shudder at the very idea of spending an evening with their husbands. Men react like I'm recommending a visit to the gallows when I say, 'Why don't you go enjoy a weekend with your wife?' 'Are you crazy? What for?' couples chorus, like I've suggested something truly awful! If the thought of spending forty-eight hours together can arouse such strong feelings, how can these same people endure a lifetime of marriage? 'Lifetime' then begins to sound alarmingly like a 'life sentence'—two people doomed to live together till one of them dies.

The Truth About Marriage

I talk to my older children about reinventing romance in their relationships. They look at me like I'm suggesting a tiresome workshop. They are really puzzled. What's worse, they aren't faking it. What is romance, they ask. Is it poetry? Moonlit drives? Long-stemmed red roses? Chocolates and gifts? No, no, no, I protest. That's not romance at all. Those are clichés. Not our clichés, either, but clichés imposed on us by Hollywood at its soppiest. Sure, romance is replete with clichés in any society, but let's at least stick to our own.

My mother was not a romantic woman. I suspect she was shy. My father, on the other hand, was and remains a diehard romantic. Between Dé and my father, there's me—self-conscious about my own sentimentality and frequently paralysed by my inability to articulate my real feelings. Despite that, I recognize the power of romance, especially in mature marriages that have crossed a few significant milestones.

My father took an active interest in my mother's wardrobe—in fact, he bought every single saree she possessed. She wore his favourite colours (blue, pink, green), and shunned those he didn't approve of (yellow, purple). I don't know how she felt about wearing only those colours that pleased her husband all through their marriage (a few months short of sixty years). But I do know that, without my realizing it, I'm following a similar pattern. I rarely wear something I know Dé does not like. For one, I trust his aesthetics and know his taste. For another, I believe it's important that your partner enjoy the way you look. Unless, of course, the partner has ghastly or kinky taste. In which case, a line has to be drawn at the outset. And this goes both ways. There have been times when Dé has climbed out of a pair of trousers or changed his jacket after one long look from me.

I used to find my father's deep and abiding interest in my mother's appearance most romantic. He picked her 'scent' (it was always 'scent', never 'perfume') and decided on her jewellery. If she felt differently about these matters, she never voiced it. Both Dé and my father are a combination of the conservative and the contemporary. Both have strong opinions on all subjects—including how their wives should look.

Years ago, Dé happened to comment on how unflattering a garment the salwar-kameez is. 'It does nothing for you,' he said dismissively, minutes before we were to leave for an important function. That was it. I rushed back into our room and changed into a saree. I have not worn a salwar-kameez since then! Our friends find this strange and often comment on the 'paradox', saying they don't expect someone like me to conform to a man's image of what his wife should look like. Honestly speaking, their 'surprise' surprises me! I think it's the most natural thing to do. And there's absolutely no shame in it. Reserve your ego battles for something more important. Don't let a salwar-kameez ruin your evening.

Last year on my birthday, I was adamant I didn't want a fuss. I told Dé to go easy on the celebrations. No real reason. I just wasn't upto it. Come on, I told my family, aren't you tired of thinking up new ideas each year? Let's treat it like any other day. Hold the presents, midnight celebrations, cake cutting, everything. Secretly, perhaps, I was testing them. Would they be relieved? Would the children say to one another, 'Thank God . . . now we don't have to feel guilty . . . Mother herself doesn't want to celebrate.' Dé was unusually quiet. He looked genuinely disappointed. Come January and he goes into overdrive, planning a series of surprises that, by now, the children are so good at second guessing, it's a sweet family joke.

Anyway, this time, at midnight, we adhered to one of the regular rituals. We opened a bottle of champagne and summoned the two children who were home. After clinking glasses, he presented me with a card—not one bought in a store, but a large, hand-crafted effort, painstakingly made by him in isolation at Alibag, away from the prying eyes of nosy kids and curious staff. He'd taken the trouble to buy a range of glitter pens for the artwork. Armed with this material, he'd drawn a multicoloured bouquet on the cover in his own whimsical style. On opening the card, I discovered a happy montage of photographs cataloguing the many stages of our life together.

One of the pictures, captioned 'Farm hand', showed me at my dowdiest, in an oversized shapeless T-shirt worn over ugly lycra bicycle pants. Right next to it was one of us in Mauritius, with a telling caption. And up there, in the right-hand corner, was one taken at some glittering function. Linking all these diverse images were Dé's teasing, affectionate words.

Looking at his handiwork, I felt tears streaming down my face—no gift in the world could compare with the simplicity and truthfulness of his gesture. Yes, he'd taken me at my word and cut out the elaborate dinner, lunch, cake cutting and so on. And yet, he'd marked the occasion with a very special effort. Suddenly, my silly insistence on 'no fuss, no celebration' seemed petty and petulant. What the hell, why deny such uncomplicated pleasure to those you love and who love you in return? Chastized and also grateful, I reviewed my stance. And we celebrated as always, with all the customary trimmings.

There is something intensely reassuring about family rituals, even if they do become monotonous after a point. There are daily patterns between Dé and me that friends and kids often find annoying. We never take calls at the dining table, no matter who or what. Now, this can be a little tricky, considering we generally have three meals together, barring lunch. Breakfast is brief and unvaried—Dé has his sprouts and fruit, I have my tea and toast. But those ten or fifteen minutes are key to the rhythm of our respective days.

I can tell from the expression on Dé's face as he emerges from our room, tie draped over his shoulders, briefcase in hand, whether he's tense about an impending work situation or relaxed about his schedule. We don't chat all that much (I'm not at my best in the morning), but the brief exchange is important. Often, there is more silence than conversation at the table. But as Dé often reminds me, just that uninterrupted 'connect' is enough. We gather our thoughts, deal with domestic issues that need addressing, compare schedules, plan dinner, and then with a light touch on my arm or a jaunty 'V' sign combined with a broad grin, he's gone. Leaving me alone at the dining table, to complete my compulsive reading of four newspapers, before attacking my writing for the day. It's time I cherish, even when we are fighting and refusing to make eye contact.

The fact is, even monotony can be turned into an advantage if couples make themselves aware of 'patterns' in a marriage and start thinking of these more positively. Patterns needn't be boring even if they do become predictable, and they often function as security blankets, comforting you by their repetitive power.

Each marriage is unique and certainly, no marriage is perfect, regardless of what partners may claim. Neither is any marriage static. That's exactly what makes it so exciting. Sometimes, when I look back on all the years spent with Dé, I marvel at where all that time has gone. It's the same with friends we know, who look at one another, faces registering a mixture of horror, amusement and occasionally affection, before exclaiming, 'Can't believe we've endured each other for so long—it doesn't seem like that at all.'

Meanwhile, my mind keeps going back to a photography session I once did for a plush lifestyle magazine. One of the editors wanted an essay on marriage—a mature marriage. To go with the text, her art director came up with the idea of a portrait surrounded by falling autumn leaves with a bright orange sunset as a backdrop. I was taken aback. Why autumn leaves? Why a lurid sunset? Because, someone ventured to explain, we thought you'd paint a mellow picture of your long-standing marriage now that it's in its autumn years. I nearly choked with outrage. I love volatility in any situation—not as a constant, but as a challenge. The idea of a 'mellow' marriage did not just scare the hell out of me, it scared me to death. Mellow is passive. Mellow is dull. Mellow is dead. Marriage must spring its own surprises, even a few mild shocks. Without a little (operative word: little) friction, the silken road to bliss and bonding gets a bit blah. So, I informed the earnest young women orchestrating the elaborate shoot that I wished to look wicked and wanton, not smug and silken. The shoot did not please the bosses, but what the hell, I had a ball while it lasted!

Spouse, like marriage itself, will travel freely and fearlessly over different terrains, some of them smooth, some not. I want to examine my own marriage and the marriages of people I have known intimately, and in the process try and decode the changed rules of today's wedding vows. Through anecdotes, incidents, and my own as well as others' thoughts on the subject, I shall attempt the impossible—trying to make sense of this crazy institution called marriage. Why we need it, why we hate it, why we love it, and why the world has yet to come up with a better alternative.

Since this isn't a self-help book with authorative dos and don'ts, you aren't going to get any marriage mantras here. Instead, get ready for a longish journey that takes you to some pretty interesting destinations. How marriages work, and why they fail is essentially about love—or the absence of it. My take is simple: a marriage works if you want it to. Conversely, a marriage fails for pretty much the same reason. People ask me how I rate my own marriage on a scale of ten. I answer truthfully that there are days when the score reads twelve and other times when it doesn't go beyond a very poor, very pathetic two. If you average it out, I'd say my marriage works pretty well—and I plan to stay invested.

Have I ever considered throwing in the towel and calling it quits? Frankly, yes. Which person doesn't despair at least ten times in two decades? What has kept us going in that case? Is it just the kids? Finances? Convenience? Or something much more vital? I can only speak for myself and say with my hand on my heart that the reason I remain married to Dé is very simple—I want to be his wife. I enjoy being married to him, even when he exasperates me and I want to hit him over the head with a hefty object. I still feel a sense of anticipation and excitement at the thought of what tomorrow holds for us. Us. Not me. Most times, I think plural, not singular.

I miss Dé when we aren't together (even if I'm sulking). I rarely enjoy a meal or a movie if I'm solo. Dressing up has little meaning if he isn't around to see me (he's allowed to say I look terrible, when I do). We don't always agree on issues, even important ones. But at least I know my opinion is heard with respect. In my darkest moments, I think of life without him (going to the extent of visualizing a different home in a distant city). But underlining the worst of times is still the unshakeable belief that we're in this together. We've had some great highs, some soul-destroying lows, but what the hell—we'd still rather be with each other than anybody else. At least, that's my version. As for Dé's, you'll have to ask him!

The Truth About Marriage

One
Touch and Go
Aa gale lag jaa

I like holding hands with my husband. He also likes holding hands with me. But Dé is a little shy. Which is why, when we are in public, he offers his arm and looks straight ahead, like he's surveying a dense forest for predators. If I try and slip my fingers through his, I see his expression alter and his back stiffen. Maybe he thinks we look slightly silly at our age. And maybe he's right. But I don't really care. My children find my hand-holding habit a little embarrassing as well. Especially the older daughters who keep hissing, 'We aren't babies any more . . . please . . . we can cross the street by ourselves.' It doesn't seem to occur to my husband or children that it isn't about their ability or inability to fend off predators or cross streets safely—it's about mine! Maybe I'm terrified of being hit by a car. Maybe I need to survey dense forests for predatory creatures. Or, just maybe, I love holding their hands!

Most couples stop touching each other in an affectionate, non-sexual way—haven't you noticed? No touch, no eye contact either. How sad! Just the lightest of touches can do what a thousand words often fail to—make a person feel wonderful.

I was raised differently, though. In my family, touch was almost taboo. Like it is in most Indian families. An open demonstration of affection was not encouraged, especially after little girls had ceased to be little. Even my mother, loving as she was, rarely hugged or kissed any of her children. We didn't find this strange, since we didn't know any different. I don't remember seeing my father even putting an arm around my mother in our presence, and I grew up with the same reservations.

I'd say Dé's upbringing was similar. He continues to be somewhat reticent, especially when we are outside our home. However, we talk about the importance of touch in our lives and in the lives of our kids. These days, he frequently plants a chaste kiss on my forehead when he comes back from work. This is done with an element of furtiveness—like a schoolboy sneaking a quick kiss. On my part, I keep one eye on the kitchen door, wondering what the maids may have seen. We laugh about this, but cannot get ourselves to relax or change.

Touch, as any psychologist will tell you, is crucial. Even the young of animals wither away if not petted and stroked. So it is with humans too. A hug is the best substitute for a verbal apology. Young couples forget both—hugs and apologies. I ask newly-weds how often they touch each other out of affection that is divorced from lust. Most shrug and look puzzled by the question. I ask them whether or not they spend time just holding one another without a sexual agenda. Rarely, they admit.

Knowing each other's bodies involves much more than merely focusing on

Touch is trust. Only someone you care for and who cares for you can express emotion non-verbally, just by reaching out with love. Accept touch. And reciprocate.

obvious attributes. A person who is deeply interested in his or her partner's physicality, will invariably know all the little quirks that make that person unique—a hidden-from-view mole, a birthmark, an old scar. These discoveries happen only when the exploration is intense and thorough. Women don't always enjoy scrutiny. Remember that wonderfully written scene in the second of the Bridget

Jones films where she hides behind a duvet to hide all the 'wobbly bits'?

Men seem far less preoccupied with perfection. By and large, men are more natural with their bodies and even with bodily functions. Women hide. Men strut. Even women with the most luscious figures often confess to hating some aspect of their body to the extent of camouflaging the 'defect' or refusing to be seen naked, unless the lights are switched off. Whereas, remarkably gross fellows with hairy backsides, yucky warts, pot bellies and spindly legs have no problem lying around starkers or worse, displaying themselves unselfconsciously on a crowded beach.

A lovely girlfriend of mine told me with a happy smile that she'd finally 'made friends' with her thighs! This happened after her husband sensed her insecurity and made sure she overcame her dislike, by telling her how sexy he found precisely that part of her body. The man wasn't lying, either—he really did. And he articulated it. They've never been happier.

Here is a quick look at 'touch therapy'. How it works . . . how it helps.

- ♥ A loving touch can often make up for the harshest words.
- ♥ All touching is not sexual. There's no better way to

make up than to hold each other wordlessly.

♥ Holding hands while relaxing at home or watching TV is most therapeutic. So much can be conveyed through this simple gesture. Lightly intertwined fingers say, 'We are friends—I like you,' or 'It's good to be with you, sharing this moment,' or 'Aren't we lucky we have each other?'

♥ Touch can go any which way. If it is leading up to sex, that's simple enough to interpret. If it's just a warm, companionable embrace, that's obvious too. Make sure your partner gets the right message. I've known couples getting into arguments over the 'implications' of a hug.

♥ It's important to keep touching. This may require a little effort, since touching doesn't come all that naturally to us. We have to first break through the inhibitory wall that stops us from reaching out physically, and then learn the full use of touch therapy.

♥ Don't shrink away when your partner leans over to express his or her affection by ruffling your hair, punching your cheek lightly, stroking your upper arm or neck, or even playing with your bare toes under a table.

♥ There are more nerve-endings in your finger tips than you might be aware of. Make full use of them. A tactile person gets more out of a relationship than one who shuns physical contact.

The Truth About Marriage

Two
White Lies
Jhooth bole kauva kaate

Sometimes, friends ask me whether hundred per cent honesty is possible in a marriage, even the best, most trusting one. The truthful answer is: 'No'. And to that short response, I'd like to add a footnote: Is it even necessary?

Women frequently complain that they feel like complete hypocrites, lying their way through thirty, thirty-five, forty years of matrimony. I ask them to provide an apt meaning for 'hypocrite'. What exactly do they mean when they call themselves hypocrites? Well, they say, humming and hawing, we often pretend to like something we don't, we laugh at jokes that aren't funny, we are nice to in-laws when we hate them, we tolerate friends we cannot stand, we wear clothes that please our men, we behave in ways so totally put on, it's a wonder we don't get caught. And what's worse, we fake orgasms . . .

That's it?

No big crime there, in my book. I wouldn't call it hypocritical conduct at all. Rather, I'd say it's some amount of foolish fibbing, all of it well-intentioned. Which woman hasn't, at some point or the other, shamelessly altered her bored expression and feigned rapt attention when her husband is holding forth? It's all right. He feels good. She feels even better—after all, it's only the expression. Nobody can crawl into her mind and decipher the wicked thoughts swirling about there. Who can tell, watching the adoring look she throws her husband's way or the spellbound gaze she manages, that her mind is wandering around untamed? Remember Nancy's famous love-filled, besotted unblinking stare the media loved to mock? Or Hillary's equally dopey expression when Bill Clinton was around? Come on, ladies! You didn't fool anyone!

Hypocrisy is a dangerous word. Know why? It's a little too open-ended and vague. Who decides what's hypocritical, what isn't? It's all in the interpretation. Which person is not a little less than sincere occasionally? So long as you are aware of your own reasons for doing what you're doing, smiling or cooing or even saying things that are a bit iffy in their genuineness, it's a harmless game. It's only when the game goes out of control and grows into a nasty habit that it has the potential to actually hurt your marriage.

I was discussing 'total honesty', 'total transparency' with my husband the other evening. It was a Sunday. The girls were both out. We'd spent the day lazily (for a change), taken a long siesta, and were ready for an early dinner. As he puffed on a favourite cigar, he mentioned the travails of a much younger couple we both know and are fond of. 'That man's wife talks compulsively about her past. He's a little embarrassed when she discusses former lovers and boyfriends in public. But she insists she isn't a hypocrite and there's nothing to hide.'

I thought about the woman's attitude and concluded she had to be rather insecure to discuss old relationships and parade her conquests, besides being insensitive to her husband's feelings. This sort of 'honesty' is best reserved for private moments between two people, if that. I strongly believe that it isn't necessary for either to 'confess all' before committing to each other. What does the 'confessional' achieve, besides causing hurt, pain and suspicion? It's enough that the couple pledge to be true about their feelings towards each other once they formalize their relationship. Flashbacks providing nitty-gritties of past affairs do not serve any purpose. Love notes, letters, other memorabilia associated with ex-es should be promptly destroyed, signalling the beginning of a new life with a new partner. Yes, your future husband or wife should not remain in the dark about past relationships. At the same time, gory details needn't be paraded—unless the new relationship is based on negative feelings of jealousy, power-play and possessiveness. I don't call this route of discretionary revelation either deceitful or hypocritical. It is merely practical.

Countless women friends now lament the moment when they felt they had to 'come clean' and 'tell all'. So many years later, their husbands still throw their past at them and resort to cheap name-calling, ill-bred taunting, even threats. This despite the fact that the women may have led exemplary lives post-marriage. I asked my father why this is so, and the ninety-seven-year-old gentleman laughed. 'Men are highly possessive by nature. It's very difficult for them to accept the fact that their wife may have had a relationship with another man in the same way—even if it was years ago. A wise woman should place her cards on the table just once and then make no further reference to her past. The same rule applies to a wise man—but how many wise men are there?'

My father had a point, but the annoying truth about this delicate issue is that love and passion do not recognize reason and rationality. People feel what they feel—you can't talk anyone out of an emotion even if it sounds absurd to you. Nothing is invalid when it comes to matters of the heart. But sensitivity is something you can actually train yourself to acquire, provided you care enough about your partner.

Women love compliments—even fake ones. My father used to say, 'My dear, you are slightly prone to flattery.' At the time, I used to protest and argue. But he was right. I'm no different from most women, and I did have a soft spot for people who made me feel wonderful. 'Hypocrites,' my sister would hiss. Maybe. But did

Harmless hypocrisy involves only temporary pretence. A white lie is certainly preferable to harsh truths and aggressive words.

I feel good! This applies in a marriage as well. What's wrong with complimenting your partner, maybe even exaggerating a little? Who doesn't respond positively to those two magic words: well done? Even pet dogs and children do. I wouldn't call that hypocrisy.

A husband who pays compliments is not an idiot, nor are all his compliments necessarily fake or insincere. Maybe he wants his wife to feel happy; maybe he thinks it will improve her mood (if she's in a bad one); maybe he's looking for sex later—so what? If his intentions are positive, a little exaggeration is acceptable. Conversely, a woman who admires her husband's new tie (even if she doesn't think it's all that great) is indulging in harmless flattery. Nothing evil or manipulative about that. It's only when hypocrisy gets out of hand and becomes a pattern in marriage that trouble starts. When you feel one thing and project the opposite. When you flatter in order to gain something. There's nothing more deceptive (and potentially dangerous to a marriage) than a hypocrite with an agenda.

I have often talked to married girlfriends about their husbands and heard them say the most terrible things—really, really awful, depressing stuff—but their public masks and acts have been perfected to such an extent that even their husbands don't know their true feelings. I have also met debauched men who go on and on about how much they love their wives, even as they plan their next dirty weekend and boast about their conquests to male friends. If their wives are in the know and play along, well then, it's double hypocrisy, which is why I always study the faces of couples at parties as they gush away about the blissful state of their marriage. The more the man hugs and kisses his wife and showers her with compliments, and vice-versa, the more suspiciously I look for those telltale signs of double-speak and basic bullshit.

One man we know keeps issuing character certificates to his wife, saying she's the best, and heaven knows what he would have done without her. The two have coined sickeningly idiotic pet names for each other. Names that strangers wonder about. Anniversaries are celebrated with much fanfare and endless cuddling and kissing, while their children dutifully applaud. Most invitees are, alas, only too well aware of the man's ghastly reputation as a serial womanizer, have met his mistress and feel sorry for the wife, who has to participate in this sham year after year. Do I club this 'hypocrisy'? You bet I do.

Harmless hypocrisy is different and easy to decode. It's being nice to in-laws, even if you loathe them. You do it because you don't wish to hurt your partner by belittling his or her family. The 'nice' in this context applies only to occasional social occasions—dinners, weddings, funerals, birthdays. It would be too much to ask of even the most loving partner to endure nasties on an ongoing basis with a smile that's permanently frozen. That's tough. Worse, you may end up with ulcers.

Harmless hypocrisy involves nothing more than temporary pretence—say, praising a dish that has been specially cooked, or saying thank you for a present you're not crazy about, but hey, it's still a gift. Be gracious about it. I'm all for a little dose of hypocrisy from time to time. So long as you know and your trusting partner eventually finds out—and forgives—it's okay. But don't make it a habit. Fake, insincere or disingenuous is not the best way to be in any relationship, least of all in this, the most intimate one. However, a white lie now and again is preferable to harsh truths and aggressive words. Leave it. Drop it. Move on.

So, some points to think about:

- ♥ Harmless hypocrisy is okay. Manipulative hypocrisy is not.
- ♥ An occasional white lie doesn't hurt.
- ♥ Tell-all confessions about ex-es serve no purpose; they only cause hurt.
- ♥ Praise (with some exaggeration) is preferable to criticism.
- ♥ The 'H-word' can actually heal if applied judiciously.

Three
Spelling It Out
Yeh dil maangey more

Say it, go on. It's not that tough. Two small words. Two sweet syllables (the sweetest): 'I want . . .'

The 'want' could be for anything. From an ice cream at midnight to an LIC policy. Whatever works. And whatever the 'want', a partner has the absolute right to ask. Demand. Insist. But also remember: the other partner has an equal right to question. Refuse. Run. Seriously speaking, far too many couples fight shy of articulating their needs. Most don't do it for fear of rejection ('Why ask for something and give him or her the power to turn it down and insult me?') or from the weight of experience ('Well, in the past,

I've always been snubbed, no matter how small my request was.'). Neither rejection nor experience can be ignored. They have a nasty way of popping up in a marriage and derailing the best intentions.

Husbands sometimes lament that they're unable to keep up with a spoilt wife's constant demands, much as they'd like to. Wives claim that husbands ask for too much and give very little in return. Men vehemently challenge this by saying, 'Women expect us to be expert mind-readers. First, they don't open their mouths and say what they actually want. And then they pick a fight for not getting it. Either way, we're screwed.'

The peeved husbands definitely have a valid point there. In our society, especially, women are not encouraged to state their requirements directly or emphatically. It is considered ill-mannered and unfeminine. Since most men find it terribly hard to decode a woman's non-verbal communication (they have a big enough problem even with the verbal variety!), it leads to an impasse, with wives sulking and husbands puzzled.

'What the hell does she want? Why can't she simply tell me?' I often hear these angry words. It is definitely a 'woman-thing' or, at any rate, a 'wife-thing'. Healthy communication needs clarity and honesty. Healthy communication is also a habit worth cultivating. Many marriages fail to invest in this very basic practice, till one day both partners wake up to discover they've actually got out of the habit of speaking freely to each other. Problems frequently begin at this very elementary level.

Women, in particular, need to drop the silly coyness and game-playing of old, and learn to state their case clearly. What's the worst that can happen? The husband may say no (the instinctive response of husbands the world over). In which case, maybe the case itself has been misrepresented or is weak. If the guy says, 'I'll think about it. Let's discuss this after a couple of days,' he's perfectly entitled to that. Grant him those two days, and do so graciously. Don't jump on his back or down his throat and start nagging right away, with an annoying 'I knew you'd say that. You always do. Why can't you tell me right now? What's your problem?' The minute you utter those awful words, be sure you've weakened your case. His back will go up, he'll get that expression in his eyes (hostile, honey, in case you were wondering) and he may dig his heels in, just to show you he means business.

Conversely, if a husband says, 'I want . . .', a wife is automatically expected to say, 'Take it' without even asking what it is that he wants. Women who don't jump the minute they're instructed to, are labelled 'obstinate, arrogant, difficult'. Of course, things are beginning to change but the stumbling block continues to be the ability to say. 'I want' without stuttering, feeling shame or being apologetic.

There's no point in being self-conscious in a marriage. It wastes a lot of time. Partners who feel embarrassed to express their needs and desires end up feeling disappointed and hurt, without bothering to analyze why. Partners are not trained psychologists or psychics. How the hell can they possibly know what's on the other person's mind if it remains there?

Most of us take to feeling martyred and adopt the 'guilty till proven otherwise' approach. This is loathsome and entirely unfair. For years, I used to do the same. I expected my husband to anticipate my needs at all times. I wrongly assumed that husbands come with built-in intuition meters. 'How can he not guess what I want—doesn't he know me by now?' I'd seethe. Naturally there was a great deal of pride involved. 'I'm not going to ask, never! What will he think? I'm not a beggar. He should realize what the situation demands and just do it.'

Even the most attentive partner can occasionally misread signals—don't make an issue out of it. Instead, go ahead and say what you need to.

Well, I was in for a lot of heartburn and active resentment. Unwilling to open up and unable to express my disappointment, I'd seek refuge in my work, and withdraw completely. The poor guy would be genuinely baffled. 'What's wrong?' he'd ask, and I'd shake my head to indicate 'nothing' or say coldly, 'Why do you ask?' again expecting him to immediately interpret that and provide an instant explanation. When that didn't happen, I'd wallow in self-pity some more and feel intensely sorry for myself. ('What sort of an insensitive guy is he . . . how can he not figure it out? Can't he read my expression? Doesn't he know I'm not happy? Can't he tell from my body language? No? How can that be? He's pretty observant about other stuff . . . but not about me and my current state? God! He definitely doesn't love me, or else he'd have bothered to find out what was bugging me.')

This internal dialogue would go on for weeks on end. And the funny thing is, he would be blissfully unaware of my tumult and repressed anger! Then, one day, I said to myself, 'This is absurd. He's perfectly relaxed and happy. I'm the one who's angry and ill-tempered. He doesn't even know what it is he's done. What's the point? Let me just speak to him. If he still doesn't get it and fails to respond, I'll have to rethink my approach. But at least I'll feel better . . .'

And you know what? I did just that. It took a lot out of me. There was injured pride and several other issues that needed sorting, but once I'd decided to voice my feelings frankly, I was delivered from my self-created prison of sulks and silences. I spoke up. And my husband simply said, 'Why didn't you tell me all this earlier?' That was it!

And to think I'd agonized for months and months!

Young wives (and a few veterans) often say they feel 'shy' to tell their husbands what they want, for fear of being ridiculed. 'It sounds so childish to say, "Please give me this or that." Conversely, men say they also feel slightly silly articulating different needs. 'If my wife doesn't get it on her own and needs me to spell it out for her, then I'm really sorry . . . that's dumb. She obviously isn't paying attention or I wouldn't have to ask.'

To both, I want to say, 'It's okay to ask. Really.' Asking indicates confidence. Especially if there is a chance that the request might be turned down. Mature couples don't feel slighted if that happens. Some requests just may be badly timed or unreasonable. The thing to do is not say a flat 'no', but to take the time to explain the 'no'. Give a good reason, and it will be accepted.

So, go ahead and ask . . .

- ♥ Legitimate wants must be voiced, but make sure they are wisely timed.
- ♥ Often, valid requests get shot down because the timing is off; you can't expect a partner to pay full attention in the middle of a cricket match, for example.
- ♥ Partners are not mind-readers—spell out your requirement.
- ♥ Don't play childish guessing games—they're irritating

and time-consuming. Cut to the chase and state your case simply and frankly.

❤ Don't take it as a personal insult if your partner does not instantly jump to fulfil every demand.

❤ Wants fall into several different categories. Emotional wants are often the toughest to cater to—remember that.

❤ 'Wanting' is a two-way street. Wants can't go your way every time. Along with every 'want', there's also a 'give'.

❤ Don't let your ego come in the way of giving voice to a 'want'. Most people who suppress their wants (big or small) over a long time, end up feeling bitter and frustrated, while blaming their partners for having been insensitive to (unexpressed) desires. This is unfair.

Four
Talk Time
Mujhe kuch kehna hai

One evening, I took a boat to our other home across the harbour. It was Dé's idea that I should join him there for dinner. I didn't think it was a great idea, given my frenzied schedule during the day. Besides, Arundhati was in the middle of her board exams and I didn't want to leave her alone. 'She'll be just fine,' Dé said. And she said it too ('I'll be okay. It's cool. You go.').

Reluctantly, I waited at the jetty for the 6 p.m. catamaran to pull up alongside. All sorts of thoughts were whirling through my head, my cellphone was ringing non-stop, and I kept asking myself, 'Why am I doing this? It's the middle of the week. I've deadlines to meet. Arundhati's exams are on. Grrrrr . . . Dé is being unreasonable.' I was scowling as I took a seat and didn't really notice anyone or anything. I heard a soft voice saying hello, and turned around to glare. It was someone I sort of knew—not a friend, but one of those 'sweet' fellows one often encounters. He was on his way to meet his wife. Oh, well . . . we talked. And in the process, I discovered how desperately this man missed just that—talking! Given the nature of his job, he was required to be away a great deal. While his wife had 'adjusted' to his long absences, he felt quite lonely and said excitedly that he was looking forward to spending the next few days catching up with her life.

I was moved by his obvious enthusiasm. By the time we jumped off the boat, I had reviewed my earlier reluctance and decided I was being stupid, giving so much importance to deadlines and other work pressures when, actually, nothing was as precious as spending a relaxed evening with Dé, chatting in the garden, listening to music and enjoying a good dinner. Chatting was key. In our busy lives, how many of us find the time to talk—just talk? To express ourselves freely, without any specific agenda to discuss? Like we once did as children? Remember the time you could talk, talk, talk till your jaw literally dropped? I can still recall the physical pain of overworked jaw muscles when I finally quit chatting over the phone late at night, after having talked non-stop for more than three hours.

Where's the time to talk, I often hear. It's true. Each available slot is taken. Besides, people don't just 'talk' any more—they 'communicate'. And while they're busy 'communicating', they forget to note the essential difference between real communication and its modern-day version, which involves nothing more than a cold exchange of information. Information, mind you, not even ideas.

Analyze a typical exchange. 'What's up? Busy? Okay . . . we have to go to dinner tonight, remember? Tell the driver. Got the address? And the tickets have come for tomorrow, 6.30. Don't forget. Yes . . . yes . . . I know . . . It's Tinku's birthday tomorrow . . . The gift? Will do. Ah—the dentist's appointment. Damn. I forgot, again. Anything else? That's it, then. Talk to you later.' That 'later' never happens. Not for 'talk' at any rate. Real talk.

Fortunately, Dé is acutely aware of our mutual need to verbalize every aspect of our lives. I sometimes tend to forget or take 'talk time' for granted. Worse, I postpone it, for reasons that just aren't good enough (deadlines!). Dé tells me not to live under the dread of daily deadlines and it is he who ensures we get to talk, regardless.

It wasn't always this way, for as anyone will tell you, men and women talk differently. Initially, my idea of 'real' conversation was very different from Dé's. I used to believe that for a conversation to qualify as 'real', it had to be about emotions and emotions alone. You know . . . I feel this, I feel that, I used to feel this but now I feel that . . .

Men just don't talk the same way and frankly, it's far easier to learn 'guy talk'—it's less complicated and less difficult to figure out. Men tend to use the same vocabulary and stick to the same subject. They speak more coherently, in logical sentences that have a beginning, a middle and an end. Women's conversations go all over the place, in what appears (to men) a random manner. Other women have no problem keeping track of stray comments and linking them all up to form a coherent whole. It's a matter of semantics that you only require time to figure out. Both partners need to listen keenly and then point out where the confusion really lies. But to get to that stage, you have to fine-tune your 'talk time' and add some quality to it. This cannot be done self-consciously. That is, you can't sit yourself down and say, 'Come on, girl . . . add quality!' It is a process that evolves over the years—if it evolves at all.

An English friend (a sensitized male of a certain vintage) once said to me, 'People no longer converse . . . they perform. They are so busy "presenting" themselves to the world that the role playing rarely stops even in their most intimate relationships.' How true. Quality talk can be cultivated, provided a) you feel the need for it in the first place, b) you are ready to confront the lack of it in your own life and c) you decide to do something about it. As in most other things, awareness is important. These days, I stop myself from throwing banal sentences at Dé. Of course we have our share of domestic trivia to exchange (which couple doesn't?), but the minute I sense we are getting stuck in that groove, I try and pull us out. It isn't always possible. Which is why Alibag.

Dé has made a conscious decision to carve out time away from Mumbai at least once a week. Even if I do go there screaming and kicking, once I hop off the boat, I switch moods and modes instantly, for it is equally important to me. No phone calls. No interruptions. It's time to ourselves, for ourselves. What do we discuss? Oh, just about anything. It isn't a structured 'intellectual' conversation analyzing Kofi Annan's speech on the situation in Zimbabwe. We talk about our respective childhoods and small, forgotten incidents. We talk about old fears, new anxieties. We discuss new dreams, deal with stale nightmares. And, of course, we gossip with glee—spicy nuggets get analyzed, processed and junked. We discuss the kids and their concerns too, but not in an obsessive way. Like I said, this is our time. And it's precious.

Women can carry on about 'feelings' ad nauseam. Men can't. We might as well accept this and teach ourselves to talk their language.

Just the other day, I was thinking to myself how that one single commodity—time—has priced itself out of the market. Nobody seems to have it, or, at least, enough of it. Young working couples rarely go beyond 'Good morning . . . hey . . . what's up for you today? Oh. Oh. In a rush. Showering and running. Catch you later . . .' The entire day goes by in a blur—meetings, phone calls, decisions. By late evening, couples are too beat to indulge in anything more than quick, functional sex, before collapsing into fatigued sleep. Conversation? You've got to be kidding! SMS? For sure. But what do those messages contain? Forwarded jokes, mainly. Or a quick instruction. Smart texting and the new abridged lingo make it possible to convey quite a lot in a single truncated sentence. There's the office e-mail, of course. But who'd want to e-mail or chat online with a husband or wife when there are so many fascinating strangers out there?

I strongly feel that communicative families nurture communicative kids. If children are encouraged to talk and express themselves at an early age, if their views and opinions are listened to with attention and respect, they grow into adulthood knowing how to make the most of both time and words. They are not afraid to articulate their feelings or opinions. This is important. I grew up in a very communicative family myself. Even to this day, we continue to talk and talk and talk. Sure, we argue, sulk and fight but we also joke, share and empathize. This is what a family is about. If your partner comes from an entirely different, more formal background, it can lead to extremely trying situations and verbal roadblocks. In any case, the *need* to communicate feelings is a woman-thing. Most men are happy enough burying all non-essential (according to them) topics while focusing on non-threatening and useless (to women) subjects like sports, cars, clubs, or their careers. Try telling a man how you feel about a silly incident from your childhood, for instance, and watch his eyes glaze over.

It's important to accept that men and women communicate in significantly different ways. Women frequently look out for non-verbal signals, body language and facial expressions. They interpret and intercept conversations. It's a special talent men simply don't possess. They need to be spoon fed—given all the relevant 'data' in easy-to-digest pellets, preferably in a logical, coherent sequence. Men prefer bullet-point presentations; women go for complicated theses.

My husband tells me I look visibly disinterested in his Formula One / cigar / single malt talk. This is true. I've tried to arrange my expression differently and feign interest. I've failed. The fact that these three passions of his leave me cold must upset him mildly. But they are such unambiguously 'male' interests! After years of half-hearted attempts at accessing this hallowed space, I have now arrived at a fairly simple solution. He pursues his passions; I don't nag or crib.

Earlier in our marriage, I used to feel 'excluded'. But I didn't want to be 'included' either. Today, it's a comfortable non-issue. I know every alternate weekend from March to September is going to be a Formula One weekend. That's fine. I plan my own schedule accordingly. I no longer pout or get petulant if hours are devoted to discussing Michael Schumacher's driving skills. My mind is elsewhere, anyway.

Recognize the difference between exchanging information and sharing ideas.

So many of my women-friends are golf widows. Many others are married to men who live on airplanes or at airports. A lot of men say something similar—their wives travel too much, or spend most weekends pursuing their own hobbies. This is tough to balance, but not impossible. Several young couples I know in the neighbourhood manage their leisure hours without too much of a hassle. They form a group and hang together over weekends. Their kids become friends too, and it all works out. I have never been able to accomplish this feat, mainly because I don't belong to a 'group'. My friendships are on an individual basis. Ditto for my husband. The few people we both enjoy are fine in small doses, but I cannot see myself spending extended time 'bonding' on a distant beach. Couples who holiday together a great deal invariably end up fighting at some point. What's that they say about too much familiarity?

What does one do with a non-communicative partner? How does one break through the 'sound barrier'? It's difficult, but not impossible. First, one has to get to the bottom of the problem—why does the person choose not to speak? Is it a choice, in the first place? Or just a conditioned response? Sometimes, silence becomes a habit. A lot of times, people fear rejection and freeze. They cannot articulate their emotions because they are afraid of the reactions. Or, they've never known what it's like to speak up. Highly hierarchial families do not 'allow' junior members to voice their concerns. The only voice one hears belongs to the head of the family. If one has been raised like this, it's hard to suddenly open up and become garrulous. A sensitive partner will not force the pace but will gradually draw the other person out.

Non-communication can be unbearably frustrating for a person who desires it. Lonely women, denied access to their maternal families, often end up talking to pets (parrots, dogs, cats), unable to reach their husbands through words. There are husbands who recognize this about themselves and plead helplessness ('That's the way I am, dammit'). There are also those who think the wife is nuts to expect

anything else ('Does she think I've nothing better to do?').
It's possible to meet somewhere in between these two
extremes. 'Learning how to communicate' can form the
basis of an on-going dialogue, initiated by either.

I often observe couples in adjoining cars as Dé and I
drive to dinner. Frequently, the two in the backseat are
staring stonily out of their respective windows. Often,
they're intently SMS-ing or talking on the cellphone.
Sometimes, the husband is reading his files while the wife
nods her head to music. Fewer and fewer people actually
spend drive-time chatting, laughing or relaxing. A friend
observed that this is a relatively new development.
'Couples feel they'll be wasting precious time if they sit
around making aimless conversation. They utilize the time
catching up on news, music, business conversations.' An
accurate observation, if a depressing one.

I strongly recommend setting time aside for nothing
more taxing than a warm, friendly, casual chinwag. Make it
an integral part of your daily routine. Once that happens,
you won't find it so difficult to talk turkey when the need
to talk turkey arises. Couples who shun confrontational
conversations internalize their negative feelings. And when
you do that over a period of time, the build-up leads to
other symptoms. Rather a verbal blow-out than a bleeding
ulcer. Suppressed rage or resentment does not disappear
with time. If anything, it festers, till one day you discover

just how much there is in deep storage. It's vital to air views from time to time—that's a far healthier option than remaining in denial and pretending nothing is wrong.

I sometimes ask myself if there is something like 'over' communication. There was a phase in my life, years ago, when I used to talk my head off, non-stop. I would verbalize every stupid little development in my life and analyze it to death. Nothing was left alone. It was pop psychology at its cheeriest. If I hadn't talked about it, it hadn't happened— it was almost that bad. I must have been singularly annoying to everyone around me. There came a point when I didn't really care whether or not anyone was listening!

Fortunately, I snapped out of the phase before I lost the few friends constantly subjected to this torture. And then something equally strange happened. I withdrew completely. There was nothing left to say. And I had no desire to share a single aspect of my life with anyone. I became a first-rate listener instead. And there it stands. I love other people's stories and can't get enough of them. I tend to put a lid on my own concerns. Even with my husband. I feel it's presumptuous to assume others—even a partner—are interested in listening. Why burden someone with your tales of woe? Deal with them yourself. Better still, keep busy so there's little time to brood. Share positive aspects of your life, communicate on a level that energizes the other. Why infect your mate with gloom and doom stories only because you can't suffer them alone?

This does not apply to larger, deeper, more serious issues, of course. I'm only talking about trivia. I'm always astonished by women who can barely wait for their husbands to get back home before launching into unending stories about absconding maids, errant drivers, disobedient servants, annoying in-laws, nosy neighbours—grrrrrr. These days, it seems to cut the other way too. Men have taken to cribbing about food, laundry, expenses and other equally tiresome topics. Daily conversation rarely extends beyond arguments over flimsy issues. The villain, of course, is stress. With little time and too many unfinished tasks, couples bicker constantly, or lapse into sullen silences that soon become a permanent feature of their deadened-by-pressure marriage. Once this silence stretches into a habit, nobody misses conversation. And if you skip conversing, you skip sharing. It's as simple as that.

Conversation, in fact, can be converted into a great stress-buster, provided you get the tone and content right. Timing is everything.

In other words:

- ♥ Keep talking; over, rather than understate.
- ♥ Set time aside for meaningful conversation, not just idle gossip.
- ♥ Don't run away from giving voice to your feelings.

♥ Non-communication can become a habit. Verbalize fears and anxieties. If you can't share these with your partner, what's the relationship about anyway?

♥ Tune in to your partner's areas of interest. At least enough to be able to participate intelligently in a discussion.

♥ A wall of silence between partners leads to 'deadness'. Be aware. Share!

Five
Fight or Spite
Tu tu main main

Come on, let's face it. Which marriage survives without its fair quota of battles royale? Not even the sweetest, gentlest one. It is simply not possible. When two human beings share the same space, conflict is a natural corollary. How you resolve fights is the more important issue.

This depends on several factors, including the definitions of marriage in your two families, going back three or more generations. Is there a history of violent arguments, slanging matches, ugly scenes? Have you grown up witnessing tumultuous and terrible moments between your own parents? Or other close family members? Then, chances are, you'll tend to repeat the pattern, even against your better judgement and will. Some would put it down to a conditioned response; I'd call it a bad habit.

The sensible way of going about resolving differences is to articulate your real feelings. Not in the heat of the moment (Never! You'll regret every true word later), but once tempers have cooled and a semblance of sanity has been restored. It's not as easy as it sounds. Most people find it difficult to a) identify their true feelings and b) voice them. Even if your partner is empathetic and receptive, it's still tough sorting out issues, especially if the fight involves fundamental differences. Couples who shy away from addressing these differences end up raging within, and as we all know, internalizing anger is bad for the system. You don't want your skin to break out, or an ulcer to develop, do you?

Of course, when it comes to ground realities, the situation is not so easily managed. I should know. I've messed up so many times. As has my husband. We want to kick ourselves later, but often 'later' is already too late. The damage has been done. But is this damage irreversible? I think not, provided there is a genuine sincerity of purpose in the making-up process. For that, couples need a little distance—physical and metaphorical. You have to step aside, assess the problem, sleep over it (take your time) and then commit to solving it in the least hurtful manner. The operative word is 'least'. Fights leave residue. This is an unpleasant truth. They do. Accept that. But don't let the residue seep into your system in such a corrosive way that it leaves permanent scars.

In the early years of our marriage, we would argue about idiotic things—where to go, what to eat, how to spend the weekend, which movie to watch, even when to take a nap. We were still in the process of establishing our individual identities within the parameters of our 'joint venture' and I guess we were stupidly marking out territories like dogs in a park. Hierarchy in marriage is always fluid—there's nothing fixed about it. Couples make the mistake of apportioning permanent roles—you lead, I follow, that kind of thing.

An intelligent marriage is one that evolves, adapts and changes constantly. Accordingly, the rules of the 'Big Fight' keep changing too. In earlier days, I used to withdraw in silence, feeling intensely sorry for myself. I would sulk for hours and days, brooding over each slight (imagined or real), going over the entire horrible sequence, till I knew every frown, snarl and grimace. I'd find it hard to function normally with other people. My writing would come to a standstill. On the really bad days, I would find it hard, if not impossible, to swallow even a mouthful of food. Anger and hurt have an awful way of clogging all your systems. Unable to think, write, eat or even breathe normally, I'd spend my time seething in silence, thinking of a thousand ways to hit back. Today, I see the futility of that approach, for I realize I hurt nobody but myself. I went hungry, I couldn't sleep, I couldn't write, I couldn't do most of the things I so enjoy. Towards what end?

Meanwhile, Dé would try and make conciliatory noises after giving me a day to cool off. By then, his anger would have vanished and he'd be dying to get back to our over-communicative levels. I'd refuse to make eye contact, forget speak.

Hours would go by in a stony atmosphere, the monotony of which was broken by everyday domestic sounds of forks on a plate at meal times, phones trilling, maids gossiping, children chattering, TV blaring. Suddenly, all these background sounds would become oppressive and annoying, adding to my dark mood. I would resent every whisper, block out the music, my eyes staring coldly and fixedly at a painting I've always detested. That painting would then assume demonic dimensions. I would blame the painting for my condition. Its morbidity would get to me with an acuteness I find scary today. Freud would call it displacement. I call it plain silly. Such immature behaviour by an adult, supposedly rational woman. Imagine making a painting 'responsible' for the anger raging within!

Once my anger dissipated (given time, even the worst tantrum loses its momentum and heat), my neck muscles would relax visibly. My husband says he had taught himself to read all these essential non-verbal signals. Only then would he make his first tentative move towards a rapprochement, by tickling my nape. If I didn't recoil and withdraw instantly, he would know I had cooled off. Which happened more often than not.

Don't involve a third person in your fights. No judge can be entirely impartial, which means one of you will cry foul—leading to another fight!

Back then, we didn't think it important to review our respective positions and figure out what had caused the fight in the first place. Today, we handle our differences differently. Once the anger has disappeared and we are officially friends again, able to talk naturally and laugh at each other's jokes, we try and calmly dissect the fight by recreating the scenario, piece by piece. Of course, in the recreation, there are always two versions—his and mine. There is also failed memory and wrong interpretations. But the post-mortem helps us to bury whatever it was that had triggered the fight. And frequently, one issue leads to another and we end up resolving much more than the original conflict.

Not all arguments have happy endings. You have to ask yourself what causes the most fights in your marriage. It's important to isolate and identify the issues. Is it children?

Money? Priorities? Neglect? Cruelty? Something else? Find out and then tackle the problem headlong.

Emotional management in a marriage involves a lot of investment. Often, young couples decide rashly and too early in the marriage, that the premium is unaffordable. Elders can play a major role by convincing them to hang on—after all, market swings are natural. If the share is blue chip, the returns have to be good. Patience is a key ingredient in turbulent times. Alas, patience is one virtue that does the disappearing act when the chips are down.

My easy, one-step recommendation is deep breathing. No words. Just breathing. Once your mind shifts from harsh thoughts to just the basic act of taking air into your lungs and exhaling, somehow, somewhere, almost miraculously, the heaving chest and short, shallow inhalations alter rhythm and a certain stillness descends. At least enough to prevent you from contemplating murder, or worse, suicide!

Disagreements are inevitable. If you ask me, they are also essential. It is unnatural for couples to remain permanently in perfect sync. It also confuses kids, who grow up thinking it's not 'normal' for parents to argue or fight. Kids who are raised in such a sanitized atmosphere are ill-prepared to deal with the real world or even their own partners, who may not be the saints their own parents pretended to be.

At the same time, spite is always but always counter productive. It hurts no one but the person who harbours it. Spite is also self-defeating—at the end of the day, a spiteful person is a wretched person, wracked by bitterness and hate. I have seen marriages come apart painfully, horribly, all because of the corrosive effect of a nasty partner tormenting the other, using the worst weapon in the arsenal—vengeance. 'You did this . . . you said that . . . you . . . you . . . you . . .' It's amazing how petty people can get when a relationship sours.

I know of an educated, successful, attractive career woman who decided she wanted out of what seemed a perfectly tuned marriage with a co-professional. When the 'joint venture' fell apart, she went to the extent of writing to all their mutual friends, seeking support, as though it was a sympathy vote she needed to win a crucial election. She didn't stop at that. She went ahead and wrote to various clubs where she was the primary member, instructing office bearers not to allow her former husband to use any of the club facilities, to deny him signing powers at the club shop and refuse him a drink on his card. This notice was widely circulated, leading to a great deal of embarrassment and humiliation.

'I will finish him off,' she vowed, 'I'll destroy his career . . . I'll turn his friends into enemies . . . I'll forbid him from seeing the children.' She managed to achieve all these targets all right, but today, he has moved on to a caring, giving partner, a fabulous job abroad and a baby, too! As for her, she's fat, bored and desperately unhappy. She drinks a great deal, and her career is going nowhere. The kids loathe her and prefer to spend time with their father. Most of the so-called friends have disappeared. Even her own family shuns her. Sure, she succeeded in 'fixing' him for a while. But eventually, she was the person who got fixed.

Some people are just more spiteful than others. It's their nature. They claim they can't control the urge to settle scores, and can wait decades for it to happen. There is a childish element to such an attitude. 'You did this to me, so I shall do that to you.' Kids frequently say this while fighting. Adults should know better, but don't. Even in small, everyday hurts and arguments, there are those who scrupulously maintain a mental record and wait for the opportune moment to strike.

It is a fallacy that only women hang on to slights and get even at the first given chance. I find men have even longer memories and are capable of hanging on to grudges for years. I know men who have waited patiently for a decade or more to salvage their bruised egoes. Ancient wounds that have never healed completely continue to fester long after the main player has withdrawn from the fray. If this sounds like a corporate war waged over decades, that is what the marital battlefield has become these days.

My way of handling discord is to move away, physically and emotionally, if someone or something makes me deeply unhappy. I have always believed in the basic efficacy of blocking out unpleasant people. Life has many more options, so why not discard the negatives and concentrate on the positives? I've dealt with my share of avenging angels and devils, but it's been a one-sided affair, with little or no interest from my side. I've discovered over time that some prickly issues resolve themselves automatically, if left alone. Even people you once hated seem less loathsome, given distance. People change as well. With no real constants in life, it's wonderful to monitor the shifting dynamics of your own life, especially the one you share with your partner. I would say:

- ♥ If you must fight, do so fairly.
- ♥ Keep it clean and to the point.
- ♥ Don't confuse issues. If you're fighting about money, stick to money. Don't get children, in-laws, dogs and neighbours into it.
- ♥ Chalk out a mental plan and stick to the agenda. There's only so much ground that can be covered in one fight.
- ♥ Fight to the finish—don't leave anything unsaid. Fight till a conclusion has been reached, whichever way.
- ♥ Plan your fights—difficult, but not impossible.

♥ Keep fights private. There's nothing worse than a public brawl.

♥ Devise your own rules and don't hit below the belt, ever.

♥ Cry, if you have to. It's silly to suppress those tears—what for?

♥ Never lose control. Once you flip out, you become incoherent and illogical. You also weaken your own position.

♥ When in danger of losing control, count, or repeat a mantra. It doesn't have to be a religious chant. It could even be a multiplication table. The idea is to fix your mind on something other than the fight.

♥ Put the fight behind you permanently, once you've thrashed it all out. Don't raise the matter again, for that defeats the purpose of fighting in the first place.

♥ Be a sporting loser. If your partner has established his or her validity in an argument, be big enough to concede.

♥ Apologize, but only if you mean it. Too many people say 'sorry', but go on to repeat the same mistake the very next week.

♥ Make love. There's no better way to prove to your partner that all is forgiven.

Six
Friends and Foes
'Yeh dosti . . .'

There is a woman friend of mine whom nobody likes. I don't get it. She has been a part of my life for years and years. We hardly ever meet, the distance being daunting. But we communicate a great deal, chat over the phone, SMS, e-mail, send notes and memos. I wonder what my family has against her. Have I asked? Yes, several times, but the responses have been vague. She's just a 'chamchi'; you like her because she massages your ego; she is such a flatterer, it's embarrassing; oh, come on . . . what do you have in common? The pressure has been so constant, so relentless, I've finally decided to keep our friendship under wraps and curtail conversations.

Frankly, this bothers me. I resent giving in to pressure, though my husband dismisses it with a laugh, saying, 'If you like her all that much, why don't you meet when I'm not around?' The kids snigger and go into their mimicry routine. I find the family's attitude cruel, insensitive and unfair. But then, it cuts both ways, right? There are a couple of cronies my husband has sensibly dropped over the years, because of my allergy to them. I couldn't stand the men and said so. My own attitude was childish, churlish and entirely illogical. There was no basis to my antipathy. I just didn't like those guys, and that was it. But wait . . . did I dare tell my husband to drop them, or else? No way. I just made my displeasure known by . . . by . . . just being a bit of a bitch when they showed up. Cold vibes have a way of freezing the staunchest heart. I didn't have to say anything or do anything. Those fellows melted away quietly, the Lord be praised. My husband does meet them occasionally, but he doesn't insist on including me in the outing.

As for my poor woman friend, she has taken the hint and stays away. I feel guilty and wretched, but tell myself it's all in the interests of the family. Besides, who needs kids standing behind an unsuspecting visitor, pulling rude faces?

This has been the pattern, give or take a few exceptions, regarding friends. Most couples end up with other compatible couples. That has not been the case with us. A lot of my friends are single professionals. A lot of my husband's friends go back to his school days in Kolkata. 'Our' friends are few, and we cherish them. It's very hard to find people both partners like and enjoy equally. I would say it's virtually impossible. So, what is one supposed to do?

People say friends are for keeps. I'm not so sure. Especially after marriage. Friendships that intrude or demand too much from either partner are best shunned.

My parents never really had close friends they socialized with on a regular basis. They had each other, and they had their respective families. When we grew up, they had us. And that's how it stayed. Because of the simplicity of that arrangement, I grew up thinking friends were for kids. Once you got married, you stuck with your husband, that was it.

I'm not sure I don't feel the same way even now. However, I have seen marriages experiencing enormous strain on account of friendships gone awry. Women, in particular, invest a great deal in theirs. If, for any reason, her husband doesn't approve of a friendship, it exerts pressure on the woman to break off a relationship she may value. Is this fair? No, it isn't. But see it from both points of view. Negotiating friendships is time-consuming and can drain you emotionally. Add to that a partner's disapproval, and what chance does that friendship have?

Women in the workplace frequently befriend male colleagues, some of them married, some single, some gay. They tell me it's a constant battle at home, with their husbands reacting to phonecalls, SMSs or e-mails received from colleagues. 'We are just friends. Why can't he accept that?' the girls protest. For the same reason that they feel upset when their husbands look embarrassed and leave the room to take a call from a female colleague at 10 p.m.!

The men also insist it's just friendship. Is it? I don't really believe it's possible to sustain a deep and abiding 'friendship' between the sexes. But that's just my suspicious, wicked mind. Good friendships are based on trust, warmth and loyalty, just like a good marriage. Our resources are limited. How much can you give an 'outsider', once you're done with giving at home? Be honest and ask yourself that question.

Sometimes, other troublesome situations can arise because of friendships. Women often get possessive about their friends. And couples then have to carve up quotas. These are 'my' friends. Those are 'your' friends. And this lot is 'ours'. Most people settle eventually for 'ours', since it simplifies matters. Why argue and fight over someone who gives grief to the person you live with? Couples then devise a few basic rules. I can share one of mine with you. If someone has been impolite, rude, indiscreet or nasty with my husband, I drop that person instantly. I cannot be seen as a 'friend' of anybody who does not respect my husband sufficiently. I consider that disloyal and also, damaging to my own relationship with my partner. Similarly, if someone has hurt my feelings, my husband shuns that individual, regardless of his personal equation with the person. We talk about it, especially since, in the field I'm in, I have to process more people than I care to, on a daily basis. There have been times when I've forgotten an old wound and greeted my tormentor civilly. But not my husband. I've seen him take on the mightiest. And my heart has filled with pride and gratitude.

Individual friendships are possible, but their scope is necessarily limited. While I do know quite a few well-adjusted couples who party frequently with their respective buddies, no questions asked, it's still something that requires a lot of skill and tact. Most couples, the world over, arrive at a common list, or else they work it out so that the people who are in no-man's land are accommodated somehow.

I've figured an easy way around this annoying problem. I see my girlfriends on 'my' time, which means when my husband is out of town, or during the day, if I can carve out some time. Weekends are out. So are jaunts after 7 p.m. Recently, an old friend called to wish me on my birthday. She was driving to Pune with her girlfriend (an acquaintance of mine) for a day, and the other lady was keen on my joining them. My girlfriend laughed and said, 'Don't be silly. She'll never come. Shobhaa won't be allowed!'

When she narrated the conversation, I could hear the other woman giggling and saying, 'What rubbish! I don't believe it.' So, my friend gave her the phone and said, 'In that case, ask Shobhaa herself.' She did. And I promptly confirmed it. I don't think that woman has recovered. Now, 'allowed' is a loaded word. It isn't that I wouldn't be allowed, or even that I'd have to seek permission. But I know my husband's feelings about such excursions—and it's out of character for me to go along, anyway. But in theory, it does sound absurd.

Friends are not part of your dowry. Don't expect your partner to accept them instantly.

Excessive chumminess can lead to excessive familiarity, which leads to eventual misunderstandings and misgivings. I know of couples fighting for days because of a bully masquerading as a friend and insisting on meddling in their private life. There are basic rules even in friendship and one should adhere to them. Never call married people after working hours when they need their own time together. Avoid calling during meal times. Stay out of each other's private areas—sex and money, in particular. Above all, respect a confidence. Nosy 'friends' who pry and then carry tales to the other partner are worse than enemies. It's best to keep such people out of your lives.

While establishing your right to individual, one-on-one relationships, it's worth remembering that it's your partner who has to absorb all the reverberations. My husband does listen patiently when a girlfriend and I have found ourselves on a collision course, but I've also seen his eyes glaze over and impatience creep into his voice when I go on and on about '. . . and then she said this . . . and I said that.'

And yes—don't expect your husband to adore your girlfriends, especially school friends. You may have a shared history and many wonderful memories with these women, but think of the poor man being forced to endure their company over a seemingly endless evening. Then again, a stubborn 'my friends are my friends, your friends are yours' attitude doesn't always work. If you persist in such compartmentalizing, you'll soon find yourselves drifting in diametrically opposite directions. Then what?

Similarly, colleagues should remain colleagues— don't thrust them on your partner. There's nothing worse than smiling gamely through a long and tedious 'office get together' during which all the in-jokes and gossip goes above the partner's head. If the frequency of these after-hours sessions is anything over four a year, you're in trouble!

Don't test your partner's patience in this ghastly way. There's just so much flat beer and inane humour he or she can or should deal with!

Ponderable points:

- Avoid thrusting old buddies on an unwary mate—it could lead to an embarrassing situation.
- Wives need to keep inquisitive girlfriends out of their husband's hair, especially over relaxed weekends.
- Over-familiarity and excessive togetherness with 'friends' can lead to trouble. Most extra-marital affairs are conducted with 'best friends'.
- Partners can feel ignored and excluded from friendships that are too suffocating.
- Friends need to be accepted by both partners for the friendships to last.
- Friends should not dominate all your spare time—it's equally important to make time exclusively for your partner.
- Separate vacations, euphemistically called Bachelor Weekends or Hen's Parties, can lead to misunderstandings since ordinary inhibitions get tossed out of the window in salubrious surroundings like Bali or Hawaii.
- Flirting with a 'friend' is easier than flirting with a stranger. Most trusting mates remain unsuspecting till it's too late. After all, he or she was supposed to be a

close buddy . . . it's only a friendly game. Is it, really?

♥ Women need their girlfriends, and men need some quality 'buddy time' as well. Make sure both of you get to spend at least a couple of hours a week with friends who share the same interests—books, art, aerobics, meditation, hiking, golf, tennis, bridge, fishing, swimming, whatever.

Seven
Love vs Arranged
Pyar Kiya To Darna Kya

I have seen as many successful 'arranged' marriages, as 'love' marriages. This is, of course, a peculiarly Indian description that amuses the rest of the world. But hey, I see 'arranged' or 'semi-arranged' marriages catching on, even in the West. Perhaps people have woken up to the reality that there are no real guarantees, no safety nets, either way. You can consult the most revered astrologer, talk to the family pundit, match horoscopes for all the 'gunas' endorsed by the shastras, but if a marriage has to collapse, it will. Ditto for a marriage driven by emotion, which we so cutely call a 'love marriage'. It's a fifty-fifty chance, whichever option one takes.

Young people have figured this out, perhaps intuitively. A lot of kids today are entrusting this all-important decision to their folks—parents, relatives, even well-meaning friends. Of course, the new 'arrangement' is more open-ended and better structured. Devoid of the old 'rules', which prescribed the ghastly 'Dekho' session, the social meetings orchestrated by middle men or women these days work in a more acceptable fashion.

My father recalls his first encounter with my mother with a wry smile, so many decades later. He describes each stage as if it happened last week. How his eldest brother asked to see the 'girl' in broad daylight, and insisted on her displaying a bit of her ankles too! This was to make sure my mother was not lame, had no deformities in her lower limbs that a flowing nine-yard saree could successfully camouflage, and that she could walk unaided! The 'broad daylight' factor was to judge the exact shade of her complexion—naturally light-skinned, or caked with 'snow' and talcum powder? Fortunately, she was not asked to sing, dance or produce a culinary miracle for the guests' benefit!

Apart from this, their formal meeting, my uncle also surprised my mother's family with an unscheduled visit, during which he demanded the 'girl' be produced in an 'as is' condition, without as much as running a comb through her hair (beware! Maybe the future bride is bald and wearing a wig!).

Once she passed his scrutiny, the talks progressed to the matching of horoscopes. Alas! The family priest declared the match entirely unsuitable, insisting there was no hope for such an ill-starred couple. I understand he was 'persuaded' to reconfigure the astral positions with a few additional rupees thrown in for a fresh verdict. And bingo! The match was declared to be perfect after all. And so it was!

I often ask my father what he thinks are the two basic factors that made his marriage a success. He always gives me the same answer: 'character and abiding love'. With these comes the rest of the package. It helped, of course, that my father flipped for my mother's looks at first glance. But what about her? Did she have a choice in the matter? He insists she did and that nobody could have forced the spirited seventeen-year-old Shakuntala to marry a man she did not fancy.

What about fights? Differences? Tantrums? Of course their marriage had their fair share of all these. But beyond occasional arguments and sulks, I don't recall a day of sustained hostility or unpleasantness. If they had problems, they settled them in privacy. It was, in many ways, a great marriage, full of sharing, caring and deep understanding.

And more than that, full of communication.

One need not rule out either communication or passion in a modern-day arranged match. Recently, while in America, I met several extremely bright American Desis. I confess I was a little surprised when told that most of the young couples slaving away for their MBAs, were in fact, not the dating couples I imagined, who'd taken campus romance to the altar, but couples who'd met as strangers through family intervention. In this day and age, these kids had taken the crucial seven steps around the holy fire, without so much as holding hands before the wedding night! And here they were, some with young children, others still settling into their new lives as 'young marrieds', but nobody could possibly guess that they had opted for a conventional 'arranged' marriage out of choice. When I expressed my surprise, they drawled, 'Aaw—no big deal . . . it has worked out just great!' And so it seemed!

Arranged marriages have as much of a chance of working out as love marriages. Don't feel embarrassed about opting for the former.

In Mumbai, too, more and more children of parents I know are leaving it to mom and dad to look for the right alliance. 'My mother knows me better than I know myself,' a young man confessed, 'I trust her judgement. My dad has seen the world, he has more experience. They know what's good for me.' And these are guys in their mid-thirties, who have studied in foreign universities, dated a few girls, done the party circuit. And yet, when it came to marriage, they were more than happy to settle for a conventional, old-fashioned match. Much like their grandparents!

It was my generation that stupidly rebelled against a system that had worked perfectly well for centuries. A lot of us paid the price for letting our impulsive hearts decide who our life partners would be. No regrets. Just that I fear we were blindly following the West and taking our cues from Hollywood, just to prove to our parents how 'liberated' and 'modern' we were.

Our kids are smarter. And more realistic. They've seen too many marriages collapse and they definitely don't want repeat performances in their own lives. Force-fed on romantic drivel from countless movies, it's a generation that laughs at the old Mills and Boon version of marriage. They ache for performance and stability. If an arranged match can provide both, they're not averse to considering it.

My own girls receive proposals from suitable (!) boys, through well-meaning intermediaries. So far nothing has clicked. But at least the girls aren't scoffing. Ditto for the boys, who shrug 'whatever', which translates to 'It's okay'. Which is perhaps why I wasn't caught entirely by surprise when I met those desi young marrieds in the US.

They were refreshingly candid while talking about the methodical manner in which their parents had gone about the whole thing. The girls were all educated, attractive professionals who looked happy enough as they adapted to an entirely alien culture with an entirely alien partner.

'We got to know each other only after the wedding. But it has worked out,' they insisted. Some had had earlier relationships, but claimed that fact did not colour their decision. They'd made informed choices and expressed no regrets.

On the other hand, I also met alarmingly young divorcees (some with babies), who lamented the day they'd said, 'I do' to a boyfriend of long standing. 'We thought we knew each other so well. We were used to each other's ways, too. God knows what went wrong after we got married. It reached a point where we couldn't stand the sight of one another.' Can happen. Does happen. Love . . . passion . . . desire . . . madness . . . where does everything vanish? Nobody knows.

The worst thing about a love marriage that ends up on the rocks is that parents get all huffy and judgemental. 'We told you it wouldn't work. Did you listen? We knew he wasn't the right person. Now look where you are.' Parents in such a situation do have a point. But they also need to rise above their own feelings of outrage and false pride and provide much needed empathy to a child who has made a mistake and is going through hell.

Love marriages may be more common now than they once were in our society, but that's only because of increased mobility and access. Dating starts during the teenage years. Couples might see each other for close to a decade before tying the knot. But even such marriages can collapse, much to the parents' dismay. 'After ten long years you people still didn't know what you were doing! Ridiculous!'

Parents must avoid this harsh judgement trap and extend a helping hand to an emotionally distressed offspring dealing with a broken marriage and much else. This is a time which can only be described as wretched. I know the feeling. I've gone through it myself.

Your self-worth is at its lowest and you've never felt as desperately alone. You also feel the entire world is sitting in judgement over what is a personal and painful decision. Friends take sides, cast aspersions, play the blame game. As for foes—they gloat and chortle with glee, while trading the ugliest rumours and theories as to why the marriage collapsed.

If, at such a time, your immediate family turns its back on you too, then why call yourself family in the first place? All it takes is a little sensitivity, a little love, a little patience. I keep running into single parents trying hard to cope with a failed marriage, while presenting a tough facade. Having been there, I can identify with the emotion. No matter what anybody says, it isn't easy. Never was, never will be. Society is not known for its kindness. When the chips are down, you have just one person to fall back on—yourself!

Not every love match is similarly doomed. There are enough marriages based on great romance. Marriages that have survived all attempts to ruin them. Couples who have battled tremendous odds to be together—religious problems, caste problems, class problems, too. Yet, I fear the vulgarization of the entire love-marriage phenomenon.

At least some of the blame for this has to be shared by popular Hindi cinema. Love ke liye kuch bhi karega and similar sentiments. Nearly everyday, our newspapers run headlines about lovers caught in some hideous situation— elopements gone awry; acid attacks on women who have turned down ardent suitors; kidnappings and rapes. All this in the name of 'love'. It's not just an urban problem. These ludicrous manifestations of 'love' can be found in rural India, too! A direct spin-off of Bollywood potboilers, I'm convinced.

Marry for love, by all means. But be realistic at the same time. Marrying 'above' or 'beneath' your own level is an option only the stout-hearted should take. Even in this day and age, a large part of India is still preoccupied with caste and class. Those who attempt to cross either or both, will necessarily be up against a great deal of resistance.

To have the guts to stand up for your beliefs and marry the person you fancy, despite daunting odds, is a challenge. If, on the other hand, you are lucky enough to flip for someone you can happily take home to mother, go for it. There is no better reason to give up your independence than to be with a person you love and who loves you. But love alone is no guarantee.

Not all love-marriages pan out the way they do in Bollywood films. Keep your rose-tinted shades on if you must, but watch out for those clouds.

At the end of the day, it's back to the C-word: commitment. A couple in an 'arranged' match can fall in love later and make a success of their marriage. But someone opting for love cannot then look for the rewards of an arranged alliance.

Love is meant to overcome all odds and embrace any and every complication. Nothing quite as unrealistic or lofty is expected from a more conventional approach.

Which is why, the next time someone rolls up flashing the right credentials and with serious intent, I shall swiftly arrange a dekho session at Mumbai's all-time favourite 'dekho' venue—the old-fashioned 'Sea Lounge' at the Taj Mahal Hotel. Imagine me as a 'proper' mother-in-law! You can't? Too bad. I can!

So, love marriage or arranged marraige, which one works for you?

- ♥ 'Arranged' isn't for leftovers. Far from it. 'Arranged' is increasingly an intelligent choice. Today's CYPs (Confused Young People) are wisely leaving the decision to their parents, figuring it's a smarter option.
- ♥ Accept that wild, crazy romantic love has its season. Nobody on earth has been able to sustain it lifelong— at least, not with the same mate!
- ♥ If you opt for love, assume full responsibility for your decision. Take whatever comes with the terrain.
- ♥ Internet alliances are rapidly catching on. The success rate for those is the same, too. Marriage itself is such a matter of chance, what's wrong with an electronic middleman?
- ♥ Parents need to be super-sensitive to kids whose marriage may be under threat or heading for divorce. It's a painful period and not the best time for lectures.
- ♥ 'Arranged' has worked for centuries in India. 'Love' is

only fifty years old. And both can fail!

- ♥ 'Arranged' can progress to 'Love'. Alas, it doesn't work the other way round.
- ♥ 'Mom knows best' isn't such a dumb formula, after all. She often does!
- ♥ Jab pyar kissi se hota hai, forget reason, logic, good sense. Just go for it!

Eight
Marriage Most Foul
Shaadi aur barbaadi

We were spending a quiet weekend at our farmhouse when the phone disturbed our peace. 'Damn,' I said, reluctant to climb out of the old planter's chair parked in a corner of the patio. 'I hope it's important . . . urgent.' My husband glared—it's an unwritten rule when we're in Alibag that neither of us makes or receives 'faltu' phone calls. As he points out, it defeats the very idea of getting away from it all. Our weekdays are horrendous enough, with no less than thirty calls to process every day. Who needs these intrusions on a Sunday, especially when the weather is divine, a snakebird calls its mate from the top of a magnolia tree and the only sound is that of the wind rustling through an elegant Chinese bamboo grove?

The voice was low and steady. 'It's finally off,' the woman was saying. I didn't have to ask, 'What?' I knew. I gestured to my husband, relaxing against plump bolsters on an antique chaise longue. He gave me an instant thumbs down, with eyes raised quizzically. So, he'd obviously guessed, too. The minute I disconnected, he said, 'It was a foul marriage to start with. Your friend is better off without that swine.' I agreed. That 'swine' was getting away rather cheaply. After years of tormenting the lady with bouts of alcoholism, abuse, adultery and abject neglect, she was finally set to walk. My first instinct was to say, 'About time— you should have done this years ago.' Fortunately, I held my tongue and listened to her as she poured her heart out.

Nothing she was saying was new to me. I'd heard it all dozens of times. The only thing I had never heard before was the obvious relief in her voice. The nightmare she'd endured for two decades was finally behind her. She was free—if not legally (yet), at least emotionally. 'I'm leaving for the hills,' she said enthusiastically. 'I need the fresh mountain air to clear my mind.' Foul weather was finally giving way to fair. I wished her well with all my heart.

How many times have I heard women say, 'I wish he was dead'. The 'he' being the husband, of course. The same women have come back weeks later expressing shame, regret and guilt for making such a telling remark. Strangely, I've never heard a man say that about his wife. Which makes me wonder whether women are more cruel in these matters, or more put upon. A foul marriage is humanity's worst curse. A foul marriage with children is hell itself—especially for the children.

Living through a spell of 'foul weather' in a marriage is one thing; living with a 'foul person' quite another.

How foul is foul? I'd say a marriage that offers zero hope for either partner, a marriage steeped in ugliness and rancour, a marriage that has hate written all over it—my God, the answer's obvious. Call it quits and move on. The problem, of course, lies in the definition. What is 'foul'? Is there Bearable Foul vs Intolerable Foul? Can foul became fair if the two people involved work on it? Difficult, whichever way you assess the situation. I've heard horror stories that have made me wonder why on earth the marriage was on—what was in it for either?

Someone I know rather well narrated incidents that made my hair stand on end. 'Why do you put up with it?' I asked. And she replied, 'What choice do I have?' I'm sorry, but that line doesn't work for me. I believe every individual has a choice—every able-bodied, educated, self-respecting individual, that is. This lady happened to be all three and yet she insisted she had 'no choice'. So, how bad was it for her?

Well, she had incredibly cross in-laws to deal with, for starters. A father-in-law who'd made passes at her from the marriage mandap itself, and a mother-in-law who was so suspicious and possessive about her domain (the kitchen and the tijori) that she frequently locked her daughter-in-law out so as to take a thorough inventory. Food was rationed as well, with this woman sternly reminded that it wasn't her father's home and that in her in-laws' place, there was a 'system' regarding meals, with rationed chappatis and rice only thrice a week! Her in-laws were affluent, upper-middle-class businesspeople. Her mother-in-law ran an independent business, drove her own car and entertained frequently. As for her husband (whom she'd met at university in the United States), he'd metamorphosed into an unfeeling monster. As she put it, 'He raises his hand against me if I contradict anything he says . . .'

Since my friend had given up her lucrative bank job at her in-laws' request, she had to beg for pocket money, which was denied to her more often than not. Domestics were ordered not to take instructions from anyone other than the mother-in-law, and access to most areas of their large apartment was denied to her. She couldn't make or take calls without permission. Naturally, a 'no visitors' rule was enforced strictly and, worse, the charming, easy-going man she'd fallen in love with at grad school was now an abusive, overweight, hard-drinking animal. Yet, the young woman didn't want out.

I've met men with comparable grouses as well. In fact, a neighbour has started a movement demanding liberation from tyrannical women. It's an association that's growing rapidly, with a well-defined agenda that calls for a less biased approach to domestic cruelty. This man claims he used to be beaten black and blue by his wife, till one day he ran away. The woman gave chase, caught up with him and hammered the hell out of the poor fellow for daring to abandon her! I run into the man from time to time—he has finally broken free, filed for divorce and started a new life as a militant, agitating for a better life for men like himself. I'm amazed at the astonishing number of male victims who have signed up.

When I think 'foul', I think 'abuse'—physical, psychological, verbal, spiritual, mental. Nobody has the right to deny another individual his or her rights. Not even under the pretext of that most misrepresented term, 'adjustment'. Adjustment is a loaded word. What adjustment? Who is deciding this adjustment? Who gains from it? Who loses? When I hear parents of young girls saying, 'We've brought up our daughter in such a way, she'll be able to adjust anywhere,' I immediately think of a collapsible ladder or a reclining chair whose backrest can be suitably 'adjusted' to the user's convenience. Please, don't adjust, I plead mentally, on behalf of the young girl, if your parents mean what I think they do. We Indians have a peculiar notion of marital adjustment. Once a daughter is given in marriage, she is supposed to turn into an amoeba and assume any which shape her husband's family expects, even demands. If she fails to do so, fingers are pointed at her upbringing. 'What to do? Her parents didn't teach her how to adjust.'

The current generation has not been spared this kind of brainwashing, either. I've seen heiresses who were packed off to their in-laws' home with just one strong message ringing in their ears: ADJUST. Well, most of them tried and gave up after a half-hearted attempt. 'Wasn't worth the effort,' a twenty-two-year-old jewellery designer told me. 'All I had to do was feign obedience at all times. After a few months, I asked myself why I was doing it. I didn't even respect those people!'

I recall stories my mother used to tell me when I was a teenager. Stories involving members of her own family. We're talking of the previous century now—way back in the 1930s. I remember one particularly awful story of a young bride being accused of witchcraft and tortured by her in-laws, who refused to acknowledge the nineteen-year-old's independent spirit and insisted on branding her a 'chudail' because she couldn't be 'tamed'. Everybody was a part of that ghostly conspiracy, the bride's older sisters-in-law included. Finally, unable to take the torment any more, she ran away, leaving her infant child behind. Her body was found a few days later, hanging from a banyan tree outside the village.

Women in similar (but urban) circumstances frequently meet me to seek advice. 'Not all of us are bold enough to take stock and walk out,' they say. It's never easy to end a nasty marriage (or any marriage). People hang in there for silly, irrational, even cussed reasons. An American girlfriend asks why she should make it easy for her partner to waltz away and marry his old girlfriend, when she herself does not have similar plans. 'But do you still love the guy— or at least care for him?' I ask. 'Don't be crazy—of course I don't. But I refuse to be nice about this. Let him go to hell. Why should I be cooperative, when he's been such an SOB?'

Does she have a point? I don't know. I don't think so. When it's over, it's over. Take stock and move on. Yes, it's difficult, traumatic and hurtful. Yes, one suffers and aches. But there's nothing more destructive than a damaged relationship you refuse to let go of—whatever the reason.

Think positive; repair the cracks, marriage counsellors generally advise. Sure, give it a go, by all means. Why give up if there's even a five per cent chance of a reconciliation? But I've never seen these sort of patch-up band-aid compromises working out well. An enriching marriage is one that operates on an altogether different principle.

If you think about it, hate and love are both four-letter words. Sometimes the good one (love) can change into the bad one (hate). I have never seen it happening the other way. Hate feeds on hate. A house that breeds hate can never be recast as a 'happy home'. Be warned. And be prepared. Nobody can flower in a vitiated atmosphere. If the very air you breathe in your home is foul, how healthy can your life be as a couple? And what sort of emotional moorings can you offer children?

Marriages disintegrate for various reasons. Sometimes they fall apart by default. As my first one did. Maybe both of us had entered it at a wrong time in our respective lives. Maybe we had not thought the decision through. Maybe our expectations didn't match. Maybe we grew in entirely different ways. Maybe I was a bit too headstrong, a bit too impatient. So many years later, there's much regret about the sadness caused. People ask me now whether there were serious 'issues' involved. And whether or not I'd tried to address them. All I can say is that it was not the marriage I wanted. I could have stayed in it, and remained unfulfilled forever. Or I could have walked. I preferred to walk. It wasn't easy. Those were perhaps the

Children exposed to a foul marriage get permanently damaged. The scars rarely heal.

toughest years of my life. I was entirely alone, and quite broke. But my spirit remained strong, as I salvaged what I could and moved on.

- Abuse on any level—verbal, physical, emotional— constitutes 'foul' in my vocabulary. Tolerate it once and you're dead for life.

- Do not put up with abuse, no matter how contrite your partner is later. An abusive person rarely reforms. If you condone the first offence, chances are you'll end up in a vicious circle of abuse–adoration—more abuse–apology. Read Pakistani writer Taslima Durani's *My Feudal Lord* to get an idea of just how foul foul can be.

- Stem the rot early in your relationship. If there are basic issues involved (his alcoholism, her nymphomania, deceit on any level), deal with them upfront before total disintegration takes place.

- Leave room for negotiation—but only if you see light at the end of the tunnel. Otherwise, get smart and invest in a good lawyer.

- Forgiving an erring partner is fine, provided both people are in agreement over basic values. If the errant one makes a habit of it, either you are a gullible, naive, trusting fool, or your partner has all the money.

- Don't fool yourself that you're hanging on 'for the sake

of the children'. Most people hang on for their own sakes. Kids are convenient alibis. If you really care for their feelings, you'll either change the situation or walk out. I recommend the latter.

Nine
Divorce and Be Damned
Talaaq, talaaq, talaaq

Our society advises brides to go to any lengths to 'save' a marriage. Popular culture reinforces the sentimentality behind marriage symbols and rituals by making constant references to the power of the 'mangalsutra' and the 'sindhoor'. A woman without a red dot on her forehead used to be considered a most unfortunate woman—either a spinster or a widow. Green bangles, brightly coloured sarees, flowers adorning the hair, toe-rings . . . for centuries little girls have been raised to value these very visible signs of 'marriagehood'. Even to this day, mothers advise their daughters to 'hang in there, no matter what'. Fathers turn back daughters in abusive marriages, when they return to their maternal homes seeking shelter. Why? 'Because your place is now in your husband's home, that's where your destiny lies.' The D-Word (divorce) is still so dreaded that most middle-class parents won't utter it, for fear of attracting its malevolent power. And yet, as we all know, more marriages are breaking up now than ever before. Divorce has become commonplace, at least in our cities, where it's being viewed as a sad but inevitable part of a larger social change.

The other day, at my daughter's school, I overheard stray bits of conversation as kids analyzed a parent-teacher meeting at which there were more single, divorced parents than couples present. For these children, there was nothing surprising or shocking about this. 'Big deal,' they shrugged, saying casually, 'that's her step-mom . . . that's his step-dad . . . that's the granny . . . that's an uncle . . .' The teachers too seemed far more sensitized to the situation as they dealt with the specific problems of various kids and their complicated parental arrangements. 'Meet my step-mom,' a teenager said cheerfully, as the lovely lady smiled and tousled the young girl's curly mop. There was no tension, no self-consciousness, no defensiveness, no euphemisms. It was an upfront introduction that did not raise any eyebrows.

Perhaps this is still only a Mumbai, and more specifically a South Mumbai, phenomenon. But give it a couple of years, and the trickle-down effect is sure to follow. Urban children will necessarily have to deal with extended families, half-siblings, quarter-siblings, step-siblings. And all the ramifications built into these 'new families' representing our times.

Never discuss the dirty details with outsiders. Not even with 'well-meaning' relatives and 'best friends'. All you're doing is providing grist for the gossip mills.

Having dealt with it over twenty years ago myself, I can tell you that the sea change in attitudes towards divorce is startling. Two decades ago, divorce still marked individuals. Today, most people take it in their stride. There is no horror, disapproval or scorn—well, at least not in the concentrated form it used to be in. Especially amongst professionals, where the D-statistic is definitely on the rise, one finds a far more relaxed and sympathetic attitude towards couples who've decided to call it quits.

But with this relatively new social shift, a slightly confused and confusing scenario has also emerged. How does one deal with the ex? What does etiquette require? Should one leave town to start over again in relative anonymity? Or is it best to stick it out and work on mutually acceptable rules of conduct? A lot of couples are opting for the second option and refusing to run away from the situation. 'It's far better to arrive at an understanding and behave like mature adults who've moved on,' said a divorcee in her late twenties, who is currently dating and exploring options. 'It isn't easy since my previous husband has remarried and we do run into each other socially. But it is far better to be civil and keep communication lines open, especially if children are involved.'

There are any number of divorced men in Mumbai who feel this way about their former wives. 'Look, so what if it didn't work out between us? Those old days of name-calling and hating each other are over. Today, we chat from time to time. But also, we make sure to follow certain rules.' And these 'rules' are as revelatory as they are fascinating.

Rule number one is to respect each other's privacy. You are no longer 'answerable' to each other. Please don't demand explanations ('What were you doing clubbing with that creep last night? He's bad news—watch it.') Do not try and keep tabs or stalk your ex. It's a waste of time. An ex who has found another life, another love, certainly does not want to face a court-martial, especially from a person with whom there's no formal relationship left. It's embarrassing and unfair to all—the new individual in the picture included.

Post-divorce is a particularly trying, emotionally charged, hyper-sensitive time. A divorced person is coming to terms with several aspects of life simultaneously. Coping with loneliness, rejection, despair, pain—oh, so many complex, contradictory emotions. You may actively detest the ex, harbour strong feelings of resentment, even jealousy. You may not want to be 'nice, polite, forgiving.' The ex should understand and accept that (doesn't always happen), and back off.

All breakups are painful. Give yourself time. And demand time from an ex who may have bounced back faster and expects the same from you. It's also better to distance yourself, for a while at least. What's needed during this 'healing period' is objectivity and isolation from the source of pain. Daily contact, constant reminders or forced bonhomie do not aid the reconciliation process. The pace cannot be pushed, either. For some people, this period can be as short as a couple of months or as long as a couple of years, even decades. Others may prefer a clean, clinical break with zero contact or interaction. Enough people have told me, 'I can't handle it. I don't want to have anything whatsoever to do with my ex. This decision has scarred me for life.' So be it. If the wound remains raw and festering, the needed salve may not be a more positive relationship with the ex. But increasingly, couples are gravitating towards resolving issues in a calmer manner and arriving at some form of civilized conduct for themselves.

'I could not bear the thought of running into my ex

somewhere. I'd stopped going out completely. I'd become a social hermit, avoiding the places we used to visit as a couple. I couldn't sleep at night, worrying that I'd leave the house and spot my ex. It was terrible! I used to be paralysed. Thank God, I've got over that phobia now. I told myself sternly that this was crazy. And who was the loser? Me!'

Innumerable such accounts reveal the true nature of divorce—which is always negative and sad, no matter how one tries to dress it up. Couples who confront the many truths about themselves and are not afraid to admit their own failures are the ones who come up with healthier solutions. It is not easy to forgive someone who may have caused you immense sorrow, and physical and mental pain. We are all vulnerable, emotionally needy people in search of love and stability in our lives—this is the basic truth, no matter how much we may want to disguise it.

Of course we feel hurt, angry and vindictive, when the one person who is central to our sense of well-being lets us down—whatever the cause of the breakdown. The thing to do is to give yourself the time to *feel*—to experience the loss, pain, disappointment, rage, without camouflaging it, or denying its existence. It's easy to throw yourself into reorganizing your new life in a frenzied way. But in doing so, you are, in fact, short-changing your emotions, which need time and introspection to accept the new equation. All the suppressed feelings will remain buried for years, only to surface at some unexpected point in your life, in a way that you can neither predict nor control. The manifestation of these feelings can take several forms; stress-related syndromes are well-known. Why bring on an ulcer or worse, years after a divorce, when there are simpler ways to cope, with all the resources at your command?

Children today are far more open to the *idea* of divorce. It does not shock them as it did an earlier generation. Of course, it still hurts as much. Which child in the world does not want to grow up in a stable, loving home with both parents sharing the responsibility of rearing and caring? When that doesn't happen, kids today seem to handle the situation in a more practical manner, possibly because divorce is more prevalent and less of a taboo. Kids who come from broken homes are no longer ostracized by classmates. Neither do they feel 'freaky'. The environment has changed.

This gives more confidence to a single parent, whose concern is always the welfare of a child. I've heard really young kids, precocious due to their circumstances, reassuring a mother or a father that it's okay to go ahead and file for a divorce. 'Don't worry about us, we'll be fine. Really. It's cool. If you guys can't work it out, it's better to split now than later. We'll manage . . .'

Heartbreaking? Of course. But it does ease the burden

on adults who are going through their own hell at the same time, and may not have the strength to bolster their kid's morale. Guilt, in these situations, takes over, and life in a home wracked by warring partners becomes a traumatic battleground.

Kids who are better informed claim they 'understand' why parents split. 'Life is very hard these days,' they say, 'and we could tell things were not working out . . . the marriage was just not happening! Now that they're divorced there's much more shanti—we spend equal time with both. There's no problem about visiting whichever parent. And it's cool. We enjoy them separately far more than when they were together.'

Ground rules? Well, there's no substitute for good manners and grace. It's important (if kids are involved) to participate jointly in family functions that

Be truthful with your kids, but don't go overboard with gory personal details. Tell them only as much as they need to know.

require the presence of both parents. While you don't have to be buddy-buddy with your ex if you don't wish to, at least maintain a working relationship and a semblance of civility. Nothing upsets friends, relatives and kids of divorced couples more than open hostility and antagonism—understandable emotions at the turbulent time of the divorce. But over the years, these emotions can and must be replaced by acceptance, even understanding of what went wrong and why, without indulging in the counter-productive blame-game.

People ask me, so many years later, whether the 'trauma' of my first marital experience did not adversely affect my attitude to marriage itself. What made me decide to give it another shot? Wasn't I bitter, shell-shocked, cynical? Didn't I lose faith in the institution? Question it? Discard and damn it? Never! I was and continue to be a believer. If anything, there was much I learned about myself and my own short-comings when my first marriage didn't work out.

Yes, I did feel disappointed and disillusioned. It had been as 'normal' a marriage as ninety-nine per cent of the marriages I was familiar with. And yet, it wasn't what I'd always dreamed of. It wasn't for me. I wanted more. Expected more. And was willing to put myself on the line to get it.

Afterwards, I was more determined than ever not to make those mistakes (impatience, immaturity, false pride) ever again. I also knew in my heart and head that for my second marriage to endure, I would have to work sincerely and hard . . . not just for my own sake but for the sake of two sets of families—my husband's and mine. There were young children involved. There was much at stake and we couldn't afford to lose. It was one of the toughest decisions of my life, on one level. And the easiest on another! I instinctively knew 'This is it!' And so it has been.

More than twenty years later, I can honestly say that everybody deserves a second chance in life, and should grab it instantly when it presents itself. The reason I remarried was simple—I met the right man at the right time. And I intuitively recognized that this was the right decision, made for the right reason.

The dynamics of divorce vary greatly. Don't make the mistake of comparing yours with anyone else's. Comparisons lead to frustration and little else. Divorce is not about extracting a huge price or extorting money—it is about a swift and fair settlement of all differences, with a chance to move on in life. Easier said, I know. But if the attitude is right and the people involved stay positive, it is possible to avoid a messy, ugly, long drawn out battle that may leave one party richer in monetary terms, but definitely poorer when you consider the emotional price paid.

There is no doubt that divorce is here to stay. Without going into the 'whys' of it, let us instead find 'ways' to manage it in the best, most dignified manner possible.

Such as . . .

♥ Never bitch about the other person in public, no matter what the provocation. It only shows you in an awful light.

🐦 Work out a long-term plan for yourself post-divorce—something that makes you feel positive about yourself and keeps you too busy to brood.

🐦 Be cordial with your ex when you meet, but remember, you don't have to fall into each other's arms, either.

🐦 Be sensitive to new partners by maintaining a healthy distance from an unhappy past. It's not fair to anyone, least of all, to you.

🐦 Staying in regular contact with your ex is acceptable if kids are involved. Otherwise, it's best to make a clean break and start afresh.

🐦 Kids should never be used as bargaining chips or a courier service between warring adults. Deal with your communication needs yourself.

🐦 Former in-laws don't need to become out-laws, unless they have played a negative role in the break-up. Be polite at all times. And firm when you have to be firm.

🐦 Don't convert teenage kids into therapists and counsellors. If you're unable to deal with the trauma of divorce on your own, seek professional help.

🐦 Don't ask or expect friends to align themselves à la George Bush ('either you are for us, or against us'). Leave them to make their own decisions. It's not about taking sides, remember?

🐦 Don't suppress the fact that you're a divorced person. There's no need to. These days, divorce is seen as an unfortunate if inevitable part of modern life. You don't have to hide or feel ashamed.

♥ Step-children deserve your respect and understanding. Give them time to get used to the changed set-up.

♥ Finally, respect your own self and your decisions. Don't behave like a pathetic victim or that's how you'll be treated. Chin up and best foot forward. You have the rest of your lovely life ahead of you, honey! Enjoy it. You owe it to yourself.

Ten
First Among Equals
Pehley aap, pehley aap

Newspapers. Can you imagine couples whose daily battles begin at dawn over something as trivial as access to the morning papers? Well, I know several who have a problem with it. 'Limited access,' seethes a wife who cannot understand why she's the one who has to wait while her husband hangs on determinedly to the entire fat bunch of dailies they're both addicted to. 'He sits there with that awful superior expression, one arm resting possessively on the thick pile. I am supposed to wait patiently till he's done with scanning all the headlines. This is just not on. I've said so several times, but it hasn't changed a thing. He's mean and selfish.'

I remember laughing at this strange visual. Until I thought about how aggravating it must be for her. 'He says he has to read them all quickly since he's always in a hurry at that hour . . . as if I'm not. We both work. We leave home at the same time. He tells me to get to the office and read the papers there. Why should I do that? Why doesn't he? Then he suggests I read in the car . . . And spoil my eyesight while he preserves his own? And the worst thing is, he takes all the papers to the loo. Watch the news on TV, he says, as I wring my hands in frustration.'

My humble suggestion was instantly rejected. I advised the woman to get her own set of papers, so the day could begin on a better note. 'Rubbish! What a waste,' she snorted. 'Why duplicate something when one can share? Besides, as I point out to my husband, how many papers can he read simultaneously anyway?'

Men do not understand such logic—forget it. Of course the man can't read six papers at the same time, but he does not want to change an old habit. His wife is supposed to accept that monopolizing newspapers is his prerogative and privilege. In this department, he comes first. In other words, she gets low priority even though both are in equally demanding jobs. If anything, she has less time at the workplace than he does. I told her she was being obstinate and silly. The man's a bully in these matters, but in other, more vital areas, he can be counted on to stand by her like a rock. Why grudge him his silly morning game? I don't know if I made sense to her, but she's cribbing less these days. And she remains incredibly well informed—so I figure the problem has been sorted out.

Marriage is not a business arrangement. Don't convert it into one, with terms and conditions spelt out contractually.

In most conventional marriages, the balance is tilted in the man's favour. Only because in the old days, it was he who went off to gather firewood, look for food and generally make sure he and the family survived. Naturally, he also got the biggest piece of the cake. And so it continues. Many Indian homes still follow the practice of 'men first' when it comes to meal times. Men are served before women, regardless of age, with young boys sitting down comfortably with older members of the clan, leaving arthritic grandmoms to hobble around carrying large serving bowls of dal and subzi.

Women themselves feel awkward about eating ahead of the menfolk. I've been at homes where the young bahu has returned deadbeat and famished after a long day at work but has not dared to say she'd prefer to eat early and go to bed. It's unthinkable, say these amazing, articulate, successful chicks, as they smile and smile, ignoring their growling tum-tums, while husbands dawdle over drinks and gossip before taking their place at the table. Even women in nuclear families are conditioned to postpone their meals in deference to the husband's schedules. It's a cultural thing and will take ages to change, if it ever does.

Husbands have an equally valid grouse when they say women always place children first, as most mothers do. This emotional shift is a natural outcome that frequently leads to a major rift in marriage. Women who give kids first priority at all times make a huge mistake, since that act excludes the husband completely and makes him feel like an intruder in his own home. It's important even for the most enthusiastic mother to figure out exactly when and where to draw the line. 'When the kids are around, I don't exist . . . I get zero attention . . . I feel downgraded . . . low or no priority,' cribbed a husband of fifteen years. When I reported this to his wife, she replied, 'What nonsense. Is he a baby? My children need me. I have to supervise their homework, feed them, drop them somewhere, pick them up . . . What does he do, except sit around demanding tea and snacks or shouting at all of us for nothing?'

I suggested mildly that maybe this was the poor chap's way of seeking attention. Maybe he was feeling ignored and marginalized. She said huffily that she'd think about it, but added swiftly that she wasn't about to change her priorities in a hurry. 'I refuse to baby an adult who doesn't want to grow up and assume responsibility.' If this sounds familiar, it's because of how widespread the malaise is.

The reverse is equally true. Countless wives complain of neglect, saying their husbands are married to their jobs. 'Nothing is as important,' a corporate wife complained. 'I could be dying or depressed or plain bored, but my husband wouldn't notice—he's always focused on his next presentation or strategy session. I hardly see him! He travels so much and we socialize so much. All our free time is invested in furthering his career. When I bring it up, he gets mad at me and says he's doing it for me, for us. What rubbish! He's doing it for himself, his own advancement. It's become such a pattern now. I doubt he misses free time or those early years when we used to chill out in Goa or just put our feet up at home and watch movies. He travels like a maniac because he likes to, not because he has to. And he expects me to put my life on hold till he achieves his targets. That's not fair at all. What about my targets? I'm sick of sitting around waiting for him to come home. And you know what? When he does get home, all he wants to do is shut himself in his room and sleep!'

There are variations to this plot. But the message is the same: men are self-obsessed. Their only concern is themselves. They rarely think of their partner's comfort level. They're way too selfish about their own goals. Their number one priority is themselves.

Largely true.

But consider what is happening now that women are in equally competitive jobs and travelling as never before. A lot of stay-at-home husbands are behaving like neglected wives from another era. They sit at home and fume while the women are off aggressively seeking self-fulfilment, no matter what the personal cost. 'It's time we got to blaze our own trails of glory,' they chorus, while hubby watches Star Sports or yet another meaningless debate on the Budget, while his mind is really elsewhere. He's a bewildered and resentful creature who does not know how he's supposed to respond to his wife's success, since society has not provided him with an appropriate cue sheet. His untutored responses reveal another story—he thinks his wife's career-craze really sucks. He genuinely believes women should stay home, cook, clean and look after babies; he wants to go back to his grandfather's age when life was easier, and all grandma did was die for the welfare of the family. While he loves his careerist wife, he does not understand her priorities and why they sometimes come first. 'I'm the man of the house. I wear the pants. What's all this newfangled nonsense about working, earning, travelling, etc? You should be happy with your lot. Stay home, woman. That's where you belong.'

But does he say that? Never. It would be considered politically incorrect in these times. He'd be mocked and shunned, or so he thinks. Would he really? I don't think so.

The first man who gets up and boldly speaks his mind on the subject will be lauded and cheered by millions of other men who feel the same way but haven't dared to articulate their thoughts in public. The pressure to conform, to be considered sufficiently 'new age', to pretend they've evolved and have accepted the gender challenges of the twenty-first century—these are the pressures that are beginning to take their toll. Happiest is the man who boldly states his case. He stands naked and exposed. But at least he wears his honesty as a fig leaf. Rather that than a hypocrite who says one thing for public consumption and believes just the opposite.

Trouble in a marriage starts brewing from the first suppressed truth. Once you lie about where you stand on an issue, the obligation to keep up the pretence finally wears you down. Ditto for women. Wives who claim to be 'cool' about their husband's priorities (be they newspapers or out-of-town conferences) when, in fact, they loathe the long absences or the ill-disguised selfishness, end up becoming seasoned actresses. But how many people are aware of their ulcers and inner turmoil? 'We always come last,' they whine. You can almost hear the men snarl, 'That's right. You come last because you deserve to.'

Wives who keep putting themselves down end up staying there. If 'coming last' is an issue with you, make sure you assert yourself at some point. Don't expect your husband to second-guess your feelings. Tell him frankly that you have noticed how he never seems to place you or your needs first. And ask him how he'd feel if the situation were reversed. Better still, take the initiative and reverse the situation for a week or so—if that doesn't work as a wake-up call, go ahead and put Plan B into motion. This involves putting yourself first, regardless of the situation. It might lead to initial shock, even protests, but if you stay with the plan long enough, he'll get the message all right.

Flexibility is the key. As long as both people get to express opinions on a more or less equal basis, and to do things solely their way from time to time, it's fine.

The 'priority project' in marriage needs patience, if partners are serious about implementing it. What may appear to be a trivial, unimportant issue (newspapers!) actually hides a bigger truth. It generally indicates the hierarchy within the family. It shows clearly who's the boss. In modern marriages, that position is negotiable and interchangeable. But the old model scrupulously adhered to the 'man on top' view, never slowing down enough to question his credentials—had he earned that position of privilege in the first place?

Sometimes, I laugh when I see very young husbands lording it over their even younger wives. Everything but everything is on the guy's terms. If the family car has to be shared, it goes without saying he gets first preference—as he does in practically everything. The choicest morsels on the dining table are first served to him. He gets to eat first, of course. Why, he even gets to use the loo first, or if the family is travelling by train, he gets the lower berth while the poor wife clambers to the higher one, hitching up her saree awkwardly. In a packed car, he sits comfortably on the front seat, legs stretched out, while the others squeeze themselves into the backseat. During the mango season, it is he who gets the pick of the fruit, while his wife sucks the seed gratefully. Anything new that comes into the house, be it Diwali mithai or Xmas cake, is offered to him before the others can sample it. That's just how it is, the elderly ladies shrug. But does it have to remain that way?

Most wives reconcile themselves to accepting their husband's routine and adjust their own accordingly. They rise in time to look after his morning needs. If they don't have their own transport, they switch everything around, depending on the availability of the family car. They accept only those invitations that have been cleared by the husband, get dressed at the time specified by him, generally wear clothes he has okayed, leave the house when he's ready, come back when he decides he's tired, bored or both; switch off the light when he announces it's bedtime; plan meals that he approves of and serve them at his convenience; watch those movies or TV shows that he feels like watching . . . in other words, tailor their daily lives to accommodate his priorities. It's when wives break a few of these rules that trouble erupts. Men are creatures of habit. If a wife tries to get a husband to 'unlearn' one or two, chances are he'll rebel saying, 'But that's how I like it.' To maintain some semblance of sanity, it's important for a wife to reorient herself. Or maintain an independent schedule of her own, bearing in mind the repercussions of doing so.

I definitely enjoy pampering my husband from time to time. I like serving him first at the dining table or even waiting for him to start eating at dinner parties. When we travel, it's understood who gets to shower first—he does. But then, that also means extra sleep time for me. About grabbing newspapers and magazines or pouncing on the TV remote—I know when to step back and concede defeat. It's a no-win situation.

Who gets to decide when it comes to the big stuff? It varies. And is reasonably equal. But there are times when I flip out, and justifiably so. I remember an occasion (quite a recent one) when I was dying for him to come home since I had something important and exciting to tell him. Around 6.30 p.m. when the doorbell rang, I arranged my expression and waited expectantly for him to make eye contact and raise his eyebrows, as he generally does. It's my signal to let the dam burst and pour out whatever it is I'm dying to communicate. But this time, there was no eye contact, no eyebrow-raising. In fact, it was as if I'd suddenly turned invisible. Oh-oh. It was going to be one of 'those' evenings. Maybe there was something on his mind. The timing was all wrong. Okay. I backed off and kept mum. I could have sulked. I didn't. Experience had taught me to let it go. Wait for a better time. If it came while my excitement levels were still high, great. If not, too bad. The moment was gone, anyway. Instead, I tried to tune in and find out what was bothering him. It was so out of character for the guy to be this switched off and silent. I found out soon enough. And, as it turned out, what he was feeling hassled about was more important than my news.

Later that night I asked myself, what if I'd been equally switched off and he'd been bubbling over with something that thrilled him? Would he have put his own excitement on hold and tuned into me? Only he can answer that.

Most men automatically place themselves first. They don't mean to be so self-centred—they do it on auto-pilot. Which, in a way, makes it worse! It's always their moods, their needs, their thoughts. In other words, when it comes to prioritizing, chances are the woman has to keep her priorities on the back burner and wait for that opportune moment, which may or may not come. Had I overlooked his dark mood that evening and launched into my own monologue, I would have ruined it for both of us. This way, he was genuinely let off the hook (how was he to know?), while only I seethed silently. He was fine a few hours later. I wasn't—or else, I wouldn't be bringing it up now!

Men are not trained to detect the imperceptible changes—an altered expression in the eyes, a mouth that refuses to smile on cue, droopy shoulders that resist straightening up . . . that sort of thing. 'Why didn't you just tell me? I'm not a mind-reader,' I'm often told. Maybe. Then how come I often sense something is amiss without a single word being spoken? 'Aah, but women are different.'

So we are. And thank God for that. We are brought up thinking and saying, 'you go first,' regardless of who actually needs to. In a perverse way, that response becomes our priority. With any luck (and a few centuries from now), things might change.

Until then . . .

- ♥ Women are not supposed to have personal priorities. If you want yours to be addressed, make it clear from the start. Men don't like priorities being sprung on them when they aren't ready.
- ♥ Learn to balance individual priorities, based on need— who spends more time in the bathroom? Who takes longer to get ready? Who can't do without the

newspapers first thing in the morning?

- ♥ Keep 'priority talk' in perspective. Don't throw it at each other to score brownie points in a slanging match.
- ♥ If you can't sort it out verbally, list out individual priorities. Throw in everything, even the most trivial, stupid stuff.
- ♥ Decisions jointly taken are the best sort of decisions. But that doesn't always happen. So what? Some decisions are best left to the more competent partner.
- ♥ Small, silly clashes over 'my priorities vs yours' are not worth the arguments that ensue. When holiday plans get ruined because of clashing egoes, who loses out? Both!

Eleven
What's Mine is Mine
Dil tera, ghar mera

A lot of young marrieds ask me, 'How do you know what's yours and what's not? Is it okay to be possessive about one's stuff? Or does marriage mean sharing everything, every single thing, with your partner?'

Frankly, there is no clear-cut answer to that one. Idealism of the romantic kind says that 'two bodies become one' when they unite in marriage. If you buy into that theory, then yes, you surrender all to your partner—body, mind, soul and material possessions. I do not subscribe to that theory myself—it can get messy, even tricky, if things don't work out down the line. Besides, a certain level of possessiveness is natural in even the closest of relationships. There are a few precious 'things' that are yours and yours alone. There may be a few 'spaces' that are denied to all—partner included. I think one should respect this and not push for a 'welding'. I often read the gushing comments of celebrity couples who claim they go fifty-fifty with everything—no secrets from each other, either. Common bank account, same cupboard, same shoes (that too!), same club, same hobbies, same books, same toiletries, same credit card and so on.

'Don't you trust me?' a young wife asked her husband in my presence. She was pushing for a joint bank account from which she could withdraw as much as she wanted to, whenever. The man was visibly embarrassed as he said, 'Of course I trust you . . . but . . . but . . . I'm not comfortable with the arrangement.'

I'm with him. If one of the parties shies away, it's fine. Ditto for possessions which may or may not have any significant monetary value. If a guy loves his T-shirts and does not wish to share them with his wife, she shouldn't take it as a personal rejection. In these days of unisex dressing, club and gym gear and general blurring of gender lines, the temptation to raid each other's closets is strong. But beware! Imagine a young man walking into his favourite gym reeking of a clingy, feminine fragrance (his wife's!). Imagine him digging into his gym bag for a hair brush, deo, socks, or towel and finding them missing. Why? His wife has 'borrowed' them. Annoying!

The mera/tera, hisaab/kitaab issues should be addressed early in the marriage. Young wives who get into extended families find themselves particularly vulnerable because of the confusion of what exactly is hers—the stuff she's brought with her from her parental home? Or is she supposed to meekly hand over her personal jewellery, clothes and whatever else that has come with her, to family elders? What about her husband's possessions—are they really his to call his own, or do they belong to the whole family, to be used at their convenience, their discretion? Take the car he drives—is it his? If it is, can his bride use it? Or the laptop?

Trusting your partner is a good policy. But it's worthwhile to stay informed about your personal assets.

Does this sound trivial and unimportant? Trust me, it isn't. When a young wife from Mumbai relocated to Delhi, she took her car with her. 'God knows what the set-up is out there. Maybe they'll expect me to share the family car. I'm not used to that. I'd rather have my own vehicle.' So far, so good. Then came the question of who would pay for the gas and the driver. The mother-in-law refused, saying it wouldn't come out of the family kitty, since the car was for the young wife's exclusive use. The groom was embarrassed and said he couldn't afford the additional expense. Finally, the girl had to dip into her own savings to pay for her wheels. 'But at least this way, I'm not answerable to anyone—nobody can question me.' A stiff price for independence. But well worth it.

'My cellphone', 'my car', 'my computer', 'my suitcase', my . . . my . . . my . . . such a short and ugly word. Yet, most people get stuck on it. That 'my' can destroy an otherwise stable relationship. There are two ways to sort out the 'my' problem. Be candid, discuss the 'untouchables' in your life. Say truthfully, 'This may sound completely absurd to you, but I hate it when you borrow my phone. I can't bear to share my cologne with you. I'm possessive about my coffee mug/quilt/pillow/papad/chair/DVDs. Please leave them alone.' The other approach is to list out all the items that you want to cling to. Reveal the list and treat the whole thing with a sense of humour. If you can laugh off your neurotic dependence on an object—it could be something as silly as a lighter—it will cease to have the same value in your eyes.

A lot of marriages go through a great deal of turbulence on account of all the small stuff that ought not to matter. But when the tera/mera issues involve property or valuables, then the best policy is to be totally transparent and upfront.

I like to know in unambiguous terms what precisely is

mine. And once that is established, I like to have complete jurisdiction over it—no questions asked. I am free to trade/sell/swap/exchange/throw/gift/store, whatever. I would hate it if I were asked to explain or account for something that is mine, and mine alone. At the same time, I'm pretty cool when it comes to kids 'borrowing' any and every possession—from car to clothes, jewellery and make-up accessories. But even with the kids, morning toast, evening biscuits and dinner-time papads continue to have a 'Do not touch' sign on them.

Quibbling over petty stuff must sound so silly to those who don't. Well, it is pretty silly when you think of it, and yet . . . It is human nature to claim ownership over material things. But think of couples who fight over friends, relationships, even kids. 'She is my daughter.' 'He is my son.' 'How dare you say that to my children?' 'Don't you raise your voice with my friends.' Have you ever been in such crossfires? I have. And squirmed through the slanging matches. Loyalty is something that cannot be commodified. No parent can claim sole control or right over a kid, even if the alignments are clear. The minute you start treating a child or a friend or a relative like a bargaining chip, there's bound to be trouble. And yet, it's astonishing how many intelligent adults battle over proprietorial rights.

Of course, the tera/mera business becomes very important in the case of a separation or a divorce. Once love goes out of the window, so does basic decency—or so it would seem, going by the messy manner in which perfectly civilized couples have split. Then it's a question of getting down and dirty with fights over crockery, art objects, paintings, refrigerators, microwaves, even gas cylinders and bathroom fixtures. Who decides? The one who's the bigger bully, of course.

I know a wife who stole into her old home in the dead of the night and stripped the place of virtually everything, including imported hand towels and the well-tended house plants. All this, while her husband, kids and in-laws snored through the heist. Later, she said with a self-satisfied smile, 'Look, I'm not a thief. I only took what belonged to me rightfully. I'd paid for it all with my own money. I'd spent hours sourcing all the things—yes, the fancy hand towels, too. Had I asked for my stuff back, I'd have been made to beg for years. I know my ex—he's a really cheap swine.' Maybe she was right in showing such unseemly haste. But she left stunned acquaintances of the couple wondering whether this sort of a stealth operation was either necessary or acceptable in a civilized society. She did leave the pet poodles behind, saying they were not her buys. And she didn't walk off with a Grecian urn, because it brought back awful memories of their honeymoon!

While writing all this, I've been asking myself how one sorts out the tricky issue of ownership without going into legalities. How does one establish ownership in the first place? Can couples really sit down and catalogue all their belongings in an indisputable way, complete with price tags? When it comes to the crunch, who arbitrates? Whose word is the final one? What about gifts—expensive gifts? Is that exquisite pearl string or the hi-tech watch to be returned or kept? What about 'verbal' agreements? Do they hold any water? To this, someone might say, 'What about trust?' Sure, what about it?

When things go wrong, trust is the first thing that flies out of the window. People suffer from instant amnesia. Along with memory loss comes spite, rage and the desire to 'fix' the partner. That's when the mera/tera issue assumes ugly proportions. When peace prevails, there's no problem.

Carried away by romantic love, most couples will sing the same mushy song: 'In our marriage we belong to each other. And all our belongings are equally shared.' If that is the foundation on which you build your relationship, good for you. But in these uncertain times, my advice is, keep it clear, keep it simple. A listing of assets is not such a terrible thing to do. Make sure a lawyer has a copy too. In case you want to make absolutely sure those assets are not messed around with, in case of the early death of either partner, a will is a good idea. Remember, it should be witnessed and signed, preferably registered as well. That way, you simplify the inheritance issue, and make it easier for heirs to claim their rightful due.

Happiest are those who own nothing worth fighting over, or are so evolved they really don't care who gets what. Meanwhile, I shall guard my digestive biscuits fiercely, thank you.

- ❤ Tera/mera issues should be addressed and sorted out right in the beginning of a relationship.
- ❤ Human beings are possessive by nature. Respect your partner's exclusive right to certain favourite objects.
- ❤ Don't mock your partner for being paranoid about a possession, whether it is a laptop, a cell phone, a DVD player or a car.
- ❤ If you hate your stuff to be used by your partner, say so.
- ❤ Seek legal advice if confused about your rights and claims.
- ❤ If both partners are possessive by nature, it's best to leave each other's things alone—don't bother with sharing.
- ❤ Gifts fall into a grey area. It is presumed that something once given belongs to the recipient exclusively. Unfortunately, warring partners rarely agree on what was given and what appropriated.
- ❤ Listing individually owned possessions and agreeing on the list is not as crass as it sounds. In the long run, it could save your marriage!

Twelve
Dumbing Down
Pyar ka sauda

She was something else, this bright, well-groomed, articulate woman, holding onto the stem of her champagne flute with practised elegance, and talking animatedly about . . . about . . . ayahs, bearers, drivers, supermarkets, shampoos, yoga classes, playschools . . . you know, the standard 'I'm the perfect housewife/mom' spiel. I went along with it for close to an hour. Something was not right. She didn't convince me at all. But I couldn't put my finger on it.

I listened closely, and watched as she resolutely stuck to the 'mahila mandal' part of the dinner party. Ever so often, her eyes would dart towards the bar where her husband was holding court. She'd wave to him, looking slightly silly, and then go right back to discussing her son's potty-training and her daughter's bed-wetting. Perfectly acceptable concerns for a young mother. Then why was I getting the nagging feeling this one was faking it? Because she was!

Over dinner, the men (financial whiz kids, all) continued to discuss market volatility without bothering to note how boring they were sounding to us non-initiates. This lady was hovering around her banker-husband, filling his plate and generally fussing over him in an annoying, exaggerated way. At one point, the husband referred to some mega deal that had the stocks of some company reeling. Without looking up from her plate, the woman suddenly spoke up—boom—rattling off figures and data which, in a way, challenged what her husband had just finished expounding. There was pin-drop silence as everybody stared at her. I thought her husband would explode. Or break something. Like, her head!

She stared down at her plate, as if she herself couldn't quite believe she'd opened her mouth. Soon, other financial analysts began to engage her in a conversation that was obviously making her uncomfortable. The women, who till then had only heard her discuss nappies and gnocchi, also looked at her with undisguised surprise and renewed interest. She laughed nervously and said something like, 'Oh . . . don't pay any attention to me . . . I was only quoting something I read.' She swiftly changed the subject and the couple left soon after.

'Who is she?' I asked my hostess, who gave me a quick low-down. The woman had been her husband's colleague in the bank—his senior as a matter of fact. The usual story of love-at-work growing into marriage. Usual, except that the husband made an unusual request. Quit, he said. Stay home. Make babies. Host parties. Keep shut. And wonder of wonders, that's exactly what she did. No protests. No complaints. She became the perfect homemaker and tried to forget she'd ever been a sharp banker. Most times, she successfully stuck to her husband-assigned role. And smiled through it all. Until, at some stray dinner party, with a couple of extra glasses of champagne giving her dutch courage, she dared to break free and express an opinion on something other than the best remedy for healing measles scabs or fixing a mouth sore. Nobody knew what price she paid later. But going by her husband's thunderous reaction, I'd imagine it was a pretty steep one.

Well . . . it so happened that I caught her alone one night. And we got talking. 'Why do you play this absurd role?' I asked bluntly. 'Because that was the deal I made,' she answered truthfully. Her husband had imposed a set of crazy conditions that had effectively turned a sparkling, accomplished, intelligent woman into a docile, passive cow whose life revolved around car pools and coaching classes for her kids. 'What if you were to tell him you wanted to get back into the swing of things—work?' I prodded.

If you are a smart chick, you don't have to fake dumbness in order to make your partner shine.

'Divorce,' she stated flatly. Imagine such a scenario in this day and age. I wanted to throw up. She'd sold out. But for how long?

Dumbing down is never a solution. Never. A clever woman can play-act only up to a point before the strain starts to show. And when it does, it gets everybody. The same applies to a clever man who pretends to be a fool— but how much rarer is that! If a woman chooses to give up a career to turn fulltime homemaker, there's no problem—it is her desire to do so. If she's forced into making such a choice, there is a problem. And any husband who believes it can work long-term is deluding himself. And asking for trouble.

Recently, a silly little reporter called from one of those silly little weekend supplements that specialize in badly-written fluff. Her question had to do with successful women and the men in their lives. I wondered why successful men are never asked similar questions. The reporter touched on the topic of 'playing down' of one's

IQ in order to not give your partner a complex. Now what sort of woman would indulge in something as dumb as that? And why? For whose benefit? Society's? Does that same society pay the couple's/woman's bills?

The other extreme, the kind of woman my father would refer to as 'over smart', is equally annoying. One meets the O.S. woman constantly. She's the person who starts most conversations with a slightly raised voice and a supercilious smile. 'I always say . . .' she begins, and then goes on to 'discuss' whichever topic she has picked to bore listeners with. If her partner interrupts (or dares to disagree), she shuts him up with a sharp put-down or a raised brow. She knows everything but everything, especially if it concerns her husband's work.

I know a lady who has systematically jeopardized her husband's career by insisting on being his 'advisor'. After all, who else has his interests at heart? Who else knows his limitations? I don't want him to be bullied or exploited, she says self-righteously, each time the poor man gets the sack. She means well. She loves her husband. She genuinely believes her advice is appropriate and invaluable. She herself has never held a job and knows nothing about today's corporate culture. The information she gets about her husband's job responsibilities and problems comes directly from him. While he isn't exactly a fool, such is his abiding faith in his wife's judgement that he goes along blindly with whatever 'guidelines' she supplies.

'Ask for an increment—and tell them to make it better than last year's measly pay hike,' she goads. Or, 'Tell them to upgrade your airline ticket to business class. Why have they booked you into a third-class hotel? Insist on a five-star. Have you given them all the expense account vouchers for last month? Get a lower interest rate if you can. Listen . . . unless you ask for something, you won't get it—at least make the demand, then we'll see.'

Obviously her husband has full faith in her, for off he goes to put in crazy requests, only because his wife says he must. So many years (and jobs) later, he's still at it. Meanwhile, the wife burbles on about 'our promotion', 'our transfer', 'our office problem'.

In any marriage, there has to be a basic comfort level for both partners. This zone is what marks the health of a relationship. It is a good indicator of how well adjusted the couple are, with a reasonable margin for disagreement. If, for any reason, values clash violently, this precious zone gets seriously damaged. If the couple continue to live in a fractured emotional space, there's little scope for harmony and peace within their home.

I keep coming back to the core of the 'comfort zone' theory since I do believe it can make or break a marriage. Of course, comfort zones vary from couple to couple. For example, I could never be 'comfortable' with a man whose idea of Sunday relaxation is to lie around the house in scruffy shorts, drinking beer and eating a biryani lunch at 4 p.m. This may sound like a superficial grouse, but it definitely aggravates and invades my 'Sunday space', which I'm entitled to. On a deeper level, comfort zones are arrived at gradually, unselfconsciously, naturally. Couples don't really sit down and say, 'Okay, babe—this is my comfort zone. What's yours?' It could take ten years or more for two people to figure out what it is that works for them.

Comfort and compatibility are inter-linked. For most educated young people today, there has to be a sharing of mental space. A fact that was driven home to me when I spent a few days in my son's home in Dubai. After having survived a series of mainly ill-matched girlfriends, I was now surveying the newest crop.

What did I think? my son asked. I replied cautiously, carefully, 'Interesting . . .' Said he, with a satisfied shrug, 'At least we speak the same language, enjoy the same books and movies. Finally, I'm meeting people with whom I can share common reference points. I was sick of dumbing down.' I'm sure the ladies felt similarly, too, for I got to eavesdrop on a few conversations.

From this, I could tell how the flagposts have shifted. There is a far greater need to actively seek out mental comfort zones. No game-playing in the cerebral department. You are as smart as you want to be—why hide your brains and flash your boobs? All of which may have been unthinkable just a decade ago. I remember watching a well-endowed model/beauty queen who'd made a career out of publicizing hers, hiding her Kafka between shots. I asked her why she was being so coy about reading a classic. 'It disorients everybody,' she stated candidly. 'They expect me to be seriously dumb—and I play along.' I empathized with the girl, known more for her DD cup size than an IQ score. It must have been pretty awful for her to keep at it. Imagine living out the role of Barbie, when inside your head you are one hell of a smart, well-read, brainy chick.

My son insists this sort of stereotyping is passé. I'm not at all sure. I know two young female business journalists— bright, successful, tough—who are constantly being introduced as 'fashion/society writers' only because they dress sexy and are single. Both complain they are likely to die single, too, since the men they date cannot handle the 'contradictions'. Said one regretfully, 'I know more about their business than they do. But when it comes to social interaction, I'm forced to behave in a silly, frothy, non-threatening manner all evening. It's tiring and tiresome. But it's either that or no dates.'

My son believes he's ready for a 'serious' relationship now and that the only way for it to work is for him to respect his partner's priorities. Friends of his say the same thing. 'My wife has a very demanding job. She keeps long hours and has to travel quite a bit. I appreciate the pressure on her time and accommodate her schedules—no hassles.' Well, she's a lucky lady. Most 'modern' men claim the same thing. But often, this wonderfully understanding attitude is in theory alone. Much as they'd like to change, it isn't happening.

Sometimes, I half wonder whether it should happen at all. I mean, can it work? When was the last time you met a well-adjusted couple with both partners in highly demanding jobs that left them no real time together? And if you did meet this extraordinary couple, are they still with one another? The demands of marriage are such that you need to invest in it all the time and every day—most couples do so on auto-pilot without even realizing it. But believe me, the adjustments are there—every day of married life, in big ways and small. Within these parameters, an equation emerges, which then evolves into the comfort zone we all seek. When either partner, for whatever reason, decides to role-play, the strain gets to the other, consciously or otherwise.

Never talk down to your partner—not even in the privacy of your bedroom.

'Be yourself at all times,' I always say to my own children. For, if you can't be the person you are with the person you live with, what's the point? The real joy of a relationship is experienced when all masks are off and you reveal yourself as you truly are from within, and do so without fear of being judged or rejected. If the relationship is strong and worth anything at all, you will find unconditional acceptance eventually. If that doesn't happen—hey, thank your stars and move on. Easier said, I know. But I, for one, cannot imagine being stuck in a situation that demands non-stop role-playing, and worse— heavy-duty dumbing/numbing down.

In my mother's days, women (like children) were to be seen (selectively) and not heard. My mother, a no-nonsense, non-hypocritical woman, chose her own path pretty early in her marriage. She always spoke up, but did so in a non-offensive, non-belligerent manner that asked for a respectful hearing, not an agitated debate. But even with her strong will and spirit, she never openly challenged our father, at least not in our presence.

On his part, he didn't mock her views on world affairs, even when he was not in sync with what she was saying. My old-fashioned mother used to tell it like it was. But I knew ladies of her generation who were part of a tacit plot—their opinions were not for airing. No matter how clever they were, or how clued-in, their lips were sealed! They were taught to gaze adoringly (and silently) at their mates as the menfolk held forth. The question of challenging a male opinion never arose.

'It's not feminine to contradict a man,' an aunt once told me. 'Men don't like aggressive, outspoken women.' Well, of course they don't, I butted in. Does that mean we should keep mum even when they're talking utter crap? No jawab. Naturally.

There are times (so many! Too many!) when I feel like yelling, 'Stop right now . . . you have no idea how idiotic you guys sound. Stop that absurd bragging and get real. Listen to your own silly voices . . . please . . . spare me . . .' What do I do? I behave like my mother. And her mother before her. I keep shut. I smile a tight little smile. My eyes become glazed. But not glazed enough (I've become an expert!) to attract attention. I know (maybe they know too) that if I so wished, I could take them and their brain-dead arguments apart in less than five minutes—anybody with even a bit of common sense and dollops of confidence could. But I rarely do it. Not because I don't want to offend, but out of a sense of self-preservation. Why waste my breath and energy talking to idiots? Several women feel the same way—particularly if the idiots happen to be friends of the husband. In such a tricky scenario, the smart thing to do is to hold your tongue.

I recall spending time, years ago, with a wise and worldly woman in her sixties. She was the junior bahu of a large, traditional joint family. There's no doubt in my mind that she was by far the sharpest member of the clan, even though she wasn't very highly educated. Her money management skills would have shamed her MBA sons. As for her considerable negotiating powers, one just had to watch her operate in shark-infested domestic waters. And yet, this shrewd lady hardly opened her mouth. When she did, everyone listened, for she spoke sparingly but she spoke sense. Her husband valued her advice and opinion, but she gave both in the privacy of their bedroom. In public, she deferred to his viewpoints at all times, especially in the presence of family elders. I asked her once, how she managed to keep such a tight rein on her tongue. She replied quietly, 'Training'. That's how she'd been raised. And she wasn't complaining.

I recall her composure and dignity each time I encounter the tough-talking 'we-are-more-than-equal' young wives of today. Sometimes, it gets embarrassing when they go into a particularly hostile, combative mode and start taking on their partners in public. It's a tough call— keep quiet and risk being dubbed a 'dumb chick', or speak up and get labelled an aggressive bitch? I think one has to play it very carefully—and that goes for guys who want to be heard, as well. Seen from their perspective, there are too many predatory, intimidating women these days, who don't give anybody else a chance to be heard. Valid point. To which one can only add: speak up when you have something worthwhile to contribute or else, zip that mouth.

In other words:

- ♥ You have a brain—use it. You have a tongue—use that, too. Let your brain tell you when and where, though. It's always smarter to overuse the former and under-utilize the latter.
- ♥ Women who pretend to be dumb when they're super-smart fool no one. That's not called being clever, the nastier word for it is cunning. Nobody likes cunning people.
- ♥ Injuring a mate's ego is a malicious way of boosting your own. There's nothing more hurtful or humiliating than a person who's constantly proving a point or showing off his/her superiority.
- ♥ If you feel defensive about your partner making an idiot of himself/herself in public, it's best to be frank and discuss the problem before leaving home.
- ♥ There is no substitute for being yourself—warts and all!

Thirteen
Games People Play
Khiladi No. 1

Watch those eyes . . . the way they narrow and dart. See the body language as the couple enter a room. Look out for the words that emerge—there's a dangerous subtext in there that can grievously wound. Oh God! Stay away! It's that awful duo again. Don't you wish they'd finish those nasty games of theirs in the privacy of their own home instead of subjecting others to them? Haven't we all met such people? Victims of marriages that have lapsed into 'power game' mode: obsessive and, finally, fatal?

The worst power game in marriage involves the ego. An egotistical partner is an unpleasant partner—no two ways about it. At the risk of sounding sexist, I've found men to be far more ego-driven in a relationship than women. For centuries, wives have been conditioned to accept an inferior position within marriage. Power, in a patriarchal society like ours, has always rested with the husband—and if the wife had a problem with that, too bloody bad. That equation isn't working these days. Wives who are financially independent refuse to cave in and prostrate themselves at their patidev's feet. A strange reversal of roles has taken place, with women asserting themselves in exactly the same obnoxious way as men. And when women decide to play games, the games can get lethal. How does one recognize the point at which a marriage is sliding into this potentially dangerous terrain? And what can be done to stop the slide?

The issue is one of domination. Who's the boss? Who calls the shots? Most men like to appropriate that role for themselves. Power-sharing does not come easily to them. In fact, it's such an alien concept within the home that their initial reaction is one of bewilderment. 'It's not possible,' men say, scratching their heads in confusion. 'After all, I'm the husband. I must be obeyed.'

To an extent, I don't disagree. Not blind obedience but, certainly, respect is the very foundation of a civilized relationship. But that cuts both ways—or should. A wife who constantly challenges her husband's authority in public (and in private, too), exposes her own failings. You don't have to put your mate down (no matter what the provocation) to put your own self up. This is an old-fashioned view, agreed. But it works. This much I can state with confidence. Power games are frequently counter-productive, even in the corporate arena. Often, the person who initiates the game ends up losing in the final round. So it is in marriage.

'You can't go to that function.' 'I won't allow you to take that job.' 'You can forget about that trip you were planning.' 'You jolly well stay home and look after my mother.' 'If you don't write that letter and sign those papers, I'll cancel your credit card.' 'Check with me before you order anything from the club.' 'Who told you to take the car without my permission?' 'What? You've gone and committed to that dinner without first clearing it with me? How dare you!' 'Sorry, I can't attend—you should have asked earlier.' 'No way am I sitting through that programme. I don't care what those people mean to you.' 'You say you're embarrassed by my behaviour? Well, guess what? I have to hide my head in shame each time we go out.' 'I told you to keep your mouth shut in the presence of guests—do you know how stupid you sound?' 'Pity your family didn't teach you any better—in our home, we were raised differently.' 'How would you know? You don't have a master's in architecture, do you?' 'See, it's all a matter of breeding. Culturally, we are poles apart.' Does any of this sound familiar? If either you or your partner has uttered these words at some stage in your relationship, it's time to review the equation.

Power games arise out of a need to control the other, whether through money, facilities, property, time, emotion, or kids. Money is the easiest. The person who has it, controls the one who doesn't. Sometimes this control is exerted so slyly, the victim may not even realize the extent of the manipulation. Husbands who give 'house money' to their non-working wives are the worst perpetrators of this game. By either denying or enhancing the agreed amount, they make sure the wife stays on course and stays put.

Money as an instrument of control is nothing new, whether in marriage or at the corporate level. Wives with

Trying to be one-up on a partner displays just one thing— insecurity.

zero personal income are the worst sufferers, having to put up with daily humiliation at times. I know several society ladies reduced to 'borrowing' from generous girlfriends because of their husband's refusal to keep them in funds. Sometimes the 'borrowing' becomes an awful and unending cycle of debt, in which a woman borrows from a second friend to pay off the first and so on. Meanwhile, the husband, out of either ignorance or indifference, keeps tight control over the family budget and cross-questions his wife's every purchase. When he withholds money, she retaliates by withholding sex, which results in both withholding love. And that is what finishes the marriage, at least in spirit, if not letter.

Money is a delicate subject. Either you can be upfront, brazen and business-like about it or you can suffer in silence. Negotiating your way around money matters is a subtle art that very few master. Most women from a traditional background find it hard to haggle for their bazaar money. If this problem stays unresolved a year into the marriage, it remains unresolved permanently. It is best to deal with it frankly right at the beginning, with a transparent talk about where the money should go. In case the woman has her own income (inherited or earned), again it's best to sort out who pays for what, right at the start.

I have seen too many marriages flounder on account of misunderstandings or mistrust over money matters. Money is ugly and dirty, and it smells. But it is also necessary, alas. A man or a woman using it to crush the partner is indulging in a cruel act, especially if the partner has absolutely no means to support himself or herself.

Urban marriage is going through a major revolution based on just this one aspect of marriage—money. Men feel resentful if asked to 'support' a wife and family all by themselves. When this resentment translates into a pattern of cold-blooded control, not only over the other person's purse but also their dignity, it gets offensive. Most modern marriages collapse when marital fights revolve around money—not ideological issues or other differences.

A young couple I know constantly argue over who should top up the tank in the wife's car! Seems trivial? Not to the wife, who claims she feels exploited and abused by her husband's insistence on taking her car for his business appointments, when he has a car of his own! He rushes off to the suburbs and brings back the car with the petrol gauge showing empty. And the young wife can only seethe.

Another woman talked of just how small-minded her hugely successful husband was when it came to his precious 'things'—especially his fancy cars, which he preferred to lock up in the garage, while she jumped in and out of taxis running his chores. The excuses given were childish and unconvincing. Mainly, that she did not know how to handle the cars (even though she was a better driver than him). This may sound like a silly, trivial battle, but it's indicative of a bigger problem—possessiveness.

Men who are paranoid about their material possessions, whatever these may be, send out a negative message to their partners. A message that indicates a basic lack of trust, besides a reluctance to share. This can be the single most alienating aspect in a marriage. If a husband shuts out his wife in this crude way, what he's indirectly saying is that he doesn't consider her his equal. That he finds her unworthy of enjoying the goodies he owns. That those goodies are his and his alone. It is a typically feudal mindset which has no place in modern times.

People always look surprised when a wife challenges her husband's point of view in public.

Women who can make their way past money matters, and do so without feeling cheated or deprived, I would call smart managers. Every woman needs to know exactly what her assets and liabilities are. She needs to teach herself the simple art (or science) of reading a balance sheet and interpreting a bank statement correctly. Several educated women I know are baffled by the most elementary figures. I used to be like that, too, till one day I told myself, 'This is ridiculous. You are seriously disadvantaged. You cannot remain dependent on accountants and clerks. Sit down and try figuring out for yourself what the mumbo-jumbo means. It can't be all that tough if even an undergrad can sort out the figures.'

Once I made that decision and started applying my mind, these very figures started speaking to me. It was an entirely new language and, after a while, I actually found it exciting. I was thrilled to discover I wasn't dumb after all. Soon I could talk to my bank manager without stuttering and stammering. I could deal with minor glitches and day-to-day hassles without consulting someone in my husband's office. Why, I have now become fairly conversant even with filing my returns—a procedure that once used to tax me to the extent that I would break into cold sweat just thinking of the torture that awaited me in my friendly-but-firm chartered accountant's chamber. Hours and hours of staring stupidly at reams and reams of impenetrable nonsense would have my head spinning and my eyes watering. Nothing but nothing would make any sense. In sheer frustration, I would end up weeping . . . or, worse, giggling. This would amuse or plain infuriate the men dealing with my books. Their reaction would, in turn, bug me. It was a hopeless situation.

Well, today I'm filled with new-found confidence as I stare at the computer screen and pretend to take an informed, intelligent interest in the proceedings. My pretence works quite well, because there is a glimmer of actual understanding. Nobody can fully comprehend the mind-boggling workings of the Indian tax department. But one should be able to at least make some sense out of a simple statement that says, 'This is how much you earned in the financial year. And this is what you need to pay.'

It's the same when it comes to handling 'house money' or making joint decisions vis-à-vis significant purchases or expensive holidays. Figures speak their own complex language, which is worth learning if you wish to safeguard your interests.

Young wives these days come duly programmed. I remember a bride stating flatly in front of her astonished in-laws, 'What's mine is mine. What's his is his. But some of that is also mine. We still haven't worked out the numbers.'

By the way, the marriage is still on. It's been ten years. I met the girl recently and asked how she'd done it. 'Simple,' she said. 'I told my husband I was getting married for specific emotional and physical reasons. If I had to make a purely financial decision, it made more sense for me to stay single. If I chose to be a wife, I wanted to be treated as one. I wanted a husband who'd look after me. I wasn't about to write my own cheques and live like a flatmate. That too, a flatmate without equal rights and with a sexual duty to perform. Sorry. That wouldn't have worked for me.'

Was this arrangement working for her husband? For both of them? 'Yes,' she said happily. 'He cribs occasionally. But I've also given up a full-time career for a more relaxed, flexi-time job. I'm entitled to hang on to every penny of what I earn. He's there to make sure our creature comforts are met.'

I approve entirely. More women should speak up and define the ground rules. Too many marriages get corroded when touchy subjects (like money) are scrupulously avoided, or dealt with in doublespeak. Resentment starts to build up, eventually leading to accusations and a breakdown of healthy communication.

In a society as structured and hierarchical as ours, the biggest power games are related to caste and social position. Yes, alarming and retrograde as it sounds, even so-called 'modern' people often make disparaging references to their partner's lowly status in the caste hierarchy. Worse, a partner who comes from a less privileged social background is made to feel small in subtle and not-so-subtle ways. I've been at dinners where a wife has made fun of her husband's lack of awareness of some of the finer aspects of good living, pointedly referring to his modest growing-up years during which the poor fellow was not exposed to anything more sophisticated than a basic daal-chaval menu, which was eaten 'crudely' with fingers.

'The first time he tasted *foie gras* was a couple of years ago when I ordered it. And guess what? He nearly threw up when I told him what it was!' The man grinned sheepishly, squirmed a bit and shrugged. According to me, it was the wife who showed her lack of class by making fun of her husband over something as unimportant as fattened goose liver. Keeping a partner in his or her 'proper' place is such an ugly thing to do. Regardless of caste and class differences, intelligent couples should create bridges, not lay landmines.

A husband or a wife indulging in power games generally

exposes his or her own shortcomings and neuroses. A confident human being does not find the need to put anybody down, least of all a life partner.

Recently, at a very fancy dinner, the wife of a businessman suddenly announced to a startled group that she does not 'take orders' from anybody, particularly her husband. 'He dare not question me,' she stated aggressively. Assuming this was accurate, why announce it? The husband (smart man) converted her remark into a joke and defused a potentially explosive situation.

Speaking of my own marriage, I am guilty of making fun of my husband's Hindi. Sometimes, he lets it go. At other times, he bristles. The point is, my own Hindi isn't all that wonderful. If anything, there are several Sanskritized words he uses that I'm entirely unfamiliar with. I've asked myself, why do I do it? Is it just to tease him? Even if it is, the joke has been over for years. Is it because I feel protective—I say it before someone else can? Perhaps. Or maybe it has just become a bad habit over the years. Now, whenever he breaks into Hindi, he swiftly looks in my direction, as if to check my expression. This makes me feel terrible. I keep telling myself to stop. One of these days, I will. And then, he just might miss the barbs!

Very, very wealthy men play the power game differently, especially if they're married to very, very rich wives. Then, what follows is a game of one-upmanship—a variation on the 'mine is bigger than yours' syndrome. I've seen tycoons taking on the 'poor relatives' of their wives in a manner so offensive, it's amazing the marriages survive. I've also seen very wealthy wives treating their husband's relatives in a demeaning manner. All this is indicative of just one thing— a relationship in which powerless, innocent people become the victims of viciousness. Sometimes, when I talk to these disgruntled wives and ask why they don't address the main problem in their marriage, instead of being nasty to those in the periphery of their lives, they say they're trapped.

Insist on fair play and transparency at all times. Too many men take full control over their wife's bank balance, without revealing their own.

Nobody is ever trapped. What they mean is that they choose to stay 'trapped' because the material pay-off is far better than that which they would enjoy as single women. Even in this day and age, any number of educated, successful career women have told me they would rather remain in a bad marriage than risk being dubbed 'divorcees'. Don't ask me what they fear . . . if it's social stigma, then sorry, that is not reason enough to perpetuate an awful relationship.

By staying on in a marriage that offers nothing beyond creature comforts and a daily dose of humiliation, these women (and a few men) are merely creating an environment conducive to nasty power games, in which there never are any winners. I remember a delicate, faded beauty in her late fifties weeping inconsolably over frequent put-downs and humiliations emanating from her over-bearing husband. 'He controls everything . . . I have nothing. No money. No status. If I cry and complain, he dares me to leave him. But where can I go at this stage of my life? He mocks my helplessness and taunts, "If you have nowhere to go, then shut up and put up. I feed you, I clothe you, you have a roof over your head. It's more than you deserve. What have you given me in thirty-five years besides four useless children?"'

Looks and brains, jointly or singly, cause problems too. A wife who's a 'looker' generally makes sure her husband never forgets it. Especially in an arranged marriage where the elders have carefully selected a 'fair, good-natured virgin' for a toad-like groom. The poor girl's only recourse to feeling even vaguely pleased about her miserable life, is to make the toad feel indebted to her. Rarely does it happen that the groom is gorgeous and the girl unattractive—unless she has all the money and has flipped for the guy's looks. But even in that scenario, it is obvious who calls the shots in public. Haven't we all seen enough strutting peacocks at social functions, drab wives trailing miserably behind them? Just as we've seen stunning trophy wives throwing mega attitude with fat, paunchy, balding husbands waiting on them hand-and-foot.

Marrying someone who is almost unreal looking comes with its own pitfalls. Marrying a milk-white maiden when you yourself are coal-black, in the hope of producing 'wheatish-complexioned' kids, is again tricky. The gene pool can be really perverse in the tricks it plays. In a country like ours, obsessed with light-coloured skin, parents of eligible candidates invariably seek out mates of appropriate hues. Unfortunate, but true. In a high-profile marriage I'm familiar with, the wife has zero attributes other than the colour of her skin. Yet, it is obvious to all that it is she who calls the shots while her husband gazes adoringly at her. And their children! Here's the twist—all four of them have inherited their father's swarthy complexion. No wonder the market for those obnoxious fairness creams is growing at the rate it is. Fairness equals beauty equals success equals happy marriage. Really!

Brainy women don't have it much easier, either. And if you are brainy, good-looking and wealthy to boot, forget a hassle-free marriage. Show me one woman in history who has all three qualities and has found a perfect mate who matches her in every department? Think. Even Queen Cleopatra suffered. It's just not possible. A brainy, good-looking, wealthy man is the ultimate catch, but even he won't marry an equal. If he does, what sort of power will he be able to exercise over a woman who, technically at least, has it all?

Look around you. Think of the marriages you're familiar with through page three gossip and tabloid journalism. Pick any of the high profile marriages featured in those pages—which one would you consider equal or even well-matched? Look at Donald Trump's track record. I won't say Bill Gates (he's plain and so is his wife Melinda). And I exclude movie-star marriages of an earlier era (even then, an equal marriage would be hard to find, not counting Saira Banu–Dilip Kumar).

Power trips and power games are hard to escape. The only way to cope is to acknowledge their existence, become aware of your own tendency to indulge in them, and check the nasty tendency. The business of establishing your 'superiority' (in any department) over a life partner is self-defeating. You prove nothing. If at all, you set yourself up as a target for others to attack. Even in an office where there are strict power-structures, nothing is as unappealing as a boss who feels the need to constantly remind people who's boss. He eventually dilutes his own equity and reduces himself to a pretty pathetic person.

Self-worth—healthy self-worth—is the best protection against childish power games. If you know your strengths and can generously recognize the strengths of your partner, the marriage can grow in a positive, enriching way. If you think putting a partner down enhances your own image, it is a fallacy. Most people can see through the attempt and end up losing respect for you. Couples need to discuss even this touchy topic if they wish to lead their lives in a more equal way. The worst thing to do when faced with power games is to feel powerless. You write your own life sentence if you do!

I recommend:

- ♥ Upfrontness, even brazenness, right at the beginning of the relationship.
- ♥ If money is a key issue, it ought to be resolved at the start. Don't shy away from dealing with it.
- ♥ If financial privacy is what you prefer and want, say so. Remember, it works both ways. You can't get nosy and don't allow your partner to get nosy, either.
- ♥ Joint bank accounts and shared bank lockers aren't the best way to handle your finances. It's better to maintain separate accounts and assume full, independent responsibility for them.
- ♥ State frankly what can and cannot be shared. Possessive people do not suddenly transform into generous, benevolent darlings. Meanness is a trait that can't be hidden for long.
- ♥ If certain possessions are out-of-bounds for the partner, it's best to be specific. Say which ones and why.

Fourteen
Repeat Value
Ek baar phir

Rituals in relationships—how important are they? Rather, how boring are they? For someone like me, pretty boring. I fancy myself to be an improvisational artist who loathes monotony. But maybe, just maybe, behind the posturing lurks a creature of habit, as bound by routine as the next hausfrau. Dé is definitely hooked on ritualistic expressions of love and commitment, some of which drive me mad. He follows certain established patterns scrupulously, whereas I tend to flout rules. This leads to explosive situations, especially when we are travelling.

Dé's travel plans leave nothing to chance—every detail

is locked into place weeks in advance. His packing, even for a casual weekend to our home in Pune, is accomplished four days in advance, with several options in all departments (dress, booze, food). My packing gets done minutes before we need to leave our home to jump on that plane, train, or car. In the process, several necessities get left behind—toiletries, nightwear, lingerie, accessories. I've arrived minus saree petticoats, make-up, footwear, watch ... oh ... too many things and too many times for it to be either funny or cute. Fine, I've shrugged and said, 'Too bad. All my fault. Let's go pick up something locally ...' and got on with the trip. But not Dé. He gets distraught and angry with himself if he forgets the smallest thing. Dé is a planner par excellence; I'm disorganized and indifferent. To me, the destination and journey are more important—to hell with the details.

Many trips have started on a ghastly note on account of these differences. We generally drive to the station or airport fuming all the way and in cold silence. Of course, my sense of timing is atrocious—many are the flights we've nearly missed (or actually missed) because I've miscalculated the distance to the airport and forgotten all about peak-hour traffic. We've tried to work around this by taking two cars and meeting up midway. Nothing has worked so far. Dé feels I need counselling and ought to be in therapy to help me confront this problem. I feel he should relax and chill out. It's only a flight, after all. Missed one? Big deal—take the next.

Then there's the business of what one does on arrival. My impulse is to fling our bags down and rush out to see the place—regardless of the time of arrival. I can't wait to devour a new destination, no matter what the time is and how jet-lagged we are. I say impatiently, 'Why wait till morning? We haven't come thousands of miles to sleep! We needn't have left home in that case. We are here! Let's go!' But Dé, being wiser and more sensible, continues to unpack in a maddeningly methodical manner. Everything is put in its proper place, as though we've never left home. My stuff is flung all over the room and rarely hung up in the wardrobe. I live out of a suitcase, frantically rummaging for whatever I need till the last possible minute.

> *Give in when it comes to unimportant personal quirks that drive a partner crazy. Wet towel on the bed? Pick it up—it's a quicker solution than fighting over who should do it.*

Earlier, this would drive Dé berserk. I would urge him to find a decent bar, smoke a cigar, order his favourite single malt and wait for me to join him. Would he oblige? Certainly not. Instead, he'd glower and pace the room, his face like a thundercloud; my nervousness would increase and I'd lose time fumbling for stuff that was right under my nose. These days, I've found a simpler solution and it seems to be working: I lie in bed, calmly watching TV, as Dé takes his time to unpack. When he's nearly done, I jump into the shower and emerge bright, friendly, refreshed and ready to boogey—or sleep. My impatience to check out the place is sublimated. I keep my curiosity on hold and, by doing so, I ensure a stress-free vacation. Start on the right note— give in a little, and the rest takes care of itself.

Rituals, as I said before, play a major role in some marriages. Repetition is reassuring since the 'rules' are familiar. Rituals then become a kind of security blanket for couples who rely on habits to provide coherence and a sense of continuity in their lives. Some rituals are needed to provide a framework, especially if children are involved. Young children need reminders. And parents have to provide them via road maps.

I'm all for some key rituals, like birthdays and anniversaries, festivals and celebrations. Perhaps a few elements have altered over the years but, by and large, we've arrived at some 'constants' that work for us. We know that Arundhati's birthday is always marked by a Satyanarayan Puja at home. We know exactly what each one of our children enjoys on his or her birthday. We also know what we like to do on our special days. Rituals encourage anticipation. However, rituals can also lead to a sense of déjà vu (Oh no, not that routine all over again! How dull!).

We know a couple (much older than us) who have made rituals the very foundation of their relationship. Nothing ever varies in their lives. They plan every day, every month, in a manner so systematic, I feel stifled just listening to their accounts. And yet, I find them perfectly well-adjusted and in tune with each other's needs. And what's more, they're neither bored nor boring.

I have my own set of rituals and, yes, I don't vary them all that much either. My girlfriends tease me about the 'magic hour'—the time Dé gets home and we have tea together. Just a few months ago, an old friend (a much younger woman, newly married) called to ask whether she was interrupting my 'cheese and crackers' moment. I was puzzled. She then laughed and reminded me of a long and crazy afternoon we'd once spent at home, oblivious of the time, till I'd been startled by the doorbell and realized it was past 6 p.m. and that it was Dé.

I'd snapped to attention, handed her handbag to her and rushed into the kitchen to supervise his tea tray, making sure his cheese and crackers were neatly arranged. She had laughed her head off and said, 'God! I'm going to eat out on this one for a long, long time! Who would believe you drop everything to arrange cheese and crackers for your husband?'

Nothing has changed. Except that the c-and-c have

been replaced by healthier options: sprouts, steamed peas or something equally unappetizing. But come that moment and I switch off totally from whatever I might have been absorbed in a second earlier, to concentrate on our evening ritual. No phone calls. No interruptions. Even the kids stay away. It is our 'reconnect' time. And it's important to both of us. Only three or four times in a year am I away from home when Dé returns. On those days, he has his tea in his room, gulping it down swiftly while watching the news on TV. When I do get back, he stares balefully and complains about something trivial.

There were years in between when I used to get a bit bugged by this attitude, especially if I was in the middle of a writing project. I also used to react to his irritability, which I knew was brought on by hunger pangs (I feel peevish and peckish at that hour myself). Once, I complained to a girlfriend (who was single by choice). She was far from sympathetic. She advised me to pay more attention to his teatime requirements and not display even the slightest impatience at his demands.

'Men are like children when they get back from work—it's nothing but attention seeking. What does it cost you to indulge him for that hour? Doesn't he do that and so much more for you whenever you're feeling low or just pooped?' My eyes were opened by her sensitivity. Today I can laugh at our 'magic hour'. Trust me, laughter is the most healthy option. Who needs scowls and sulks?

Silly habits are hard to shrug off. That's what makes them silly. After a certain age, each one of us develops a set of mannerisms that annoy other people. I know I have my share of them. Couples who refuse to accommodate each other's little eccentricities get increasingly combative—and for what?

Most intimate habits (bathroom usage, for example) go back to one's childhood. While it's possible to alter or fine-tune them after marriage, very often, couples resist doing so for fear of giving up their 'freedom'. To this I say, 'Rubbish'. Freedom—that word should be reserved for the really important stuff in life. Not for something stupid like insisting on squeezing the toothpaste in the middle of the tube and claiming it is your birthright to do so. I, for one, invariably leave wet towels on our bed—a lousy, inconsiderate habit. I'm conscious of it, have tried to get rid of it, but I continue to err. I also rarely put my clothes neatly away after returning late from a dinner party. Most times, my discarded saree, jewellery and whatever else, is carelessly and untidily left on the carpet till the morning after. This is a strain on Dé.

How does one accommodate such annoying quirks? Can they be made to go away if enough pressure is exerted? So many 'quirks' later, I can tell you that quirks are forever. The trick is to make peace with them. I know I have a punctuality problem that drives Dé up the wall. But I have my own wonky logic. I'm never late for an official appointment. I'm never late for a one-on-one. I'm never late when and where it counts.

But with family, I don't always watch the clock. And, I have to confess, I do not adhere to 'social timings'. In a city like Mumbai, most people don't. Hostesses expect you to show up an hour late, unless it's a formal sit-down dinner. My reasoning ('poor', according to Dé) is simple: it doesn't matter a damn to anyone, least of all our hosts, whether we arrive at 9.30 p.m. or 10. So long as we show up, if we've accepted the invitation. It's not about making a dramatic entry; it's about taking a call on what's more important at that hour. I'd rather spend those extra minutes talking to my children as they have their dinner than hurtle off to an evening featuring two hundred of the city's usual suspects. But, with Dé fuming and perhaps a traffic snarl delaying us still further, the mood is ruined much before we get to the venue.

Have I changed? Has he? Naah. We still adhere to the familiar pattern, each one hoping the other will 'get it' someday.

So what should warring couples do in these circumstances?

♥ Use your judgement, depending on the situation. If

it's an official dinner party your husband is required to attend, make sure you get your act together well in time. If it's a formal function you've been invited to, insist on the same courtesy from him.

♥ Be sensitive to those things that do matter: a certain way of folding newspapers once you're done, not throwing your own stuff around in the other person's 'space' (like dogs, human beings too mark out their own territory and guard it fiercely. You know, my side of the bed, my chair at the dining table, my favourite sofa, my bookcase, my shoe shelf . . .).

♥ Concentrate on getting the basics right—are you upsetting your partner by ignoring a deep-seated need for something that may seem trivial to you but is anything but, to him or her?

♥ Respect rituals—provided they aren't too tedious. I know wives who absolutely refuse to 'understand' their husband's manic commitment to golf over weekends. A woman I know went into labour on a Saturday morning, thereby upsetting her husband's game. He refused to cancel, leaving her to endure the experience all on her own. Has she forgiven him so many decades later? Of course not! It's a recurring theme in their otherwise stable marriage.

♥ You can help your partner to get rid of bad habits by

showing concern rather than irritation. You can't nag someone to stop smoking. You have to give the person a damn good reason why he or she should. And reward the effort when taken.

♥ Learn to laugh at those silly, small things that make your partner unique. Rituals can even seem 'charming' if you 'up' your tolerance levels.

♥ Discuss . . . and then discard. Do so without hurting your partner's feelings.

Fifteen

The Dhak-dhak Factor
Dil to paagal hai

M.F. Husain, the last of the Great Romantics, once told me there's nothing more erotic or powerful in life than the unmistakable sound of your own heart going 'dhak-dhak' at the mere thought of someone. He was, of course, besotted by a gorgeous actress (Madhuri Dixit) then. But I don't think there has ever been a time in his nearly ninety-year-old life when his heart hasn't gone 'dhak-dhak' over an object of his desire. As India's most flamboyant painter, he is entitled to his obsessions and passions—what's an artist without a muse? But lesser mortals aren't always as blessed—especially if the heart has been pledged to someone solid but uninspiring.

Too many people settle for something substantially less than the level of romantic passion they dream about. This is one of zindagi's innumerable cruel tricks. Why short-change yourself, I ask dewy-eyed damsels in their twenties, who begin to resemble sheep-to-slaughter once their wedding vows have been taken, and the groom is a 'compromise candidate'.

One disappointed bride said flatly, 'Nothing wrong with my husband—he's a nice guy. Educated, secure in his career . . . he's good-looking as well. I can't really find fault with him. But he leaves me cold. He doesn't turn me on. I have sisterly feelings towards him.'

My heart went out to the beautiful girl with the turned down mouth. She was clearly missing the dhak-dhak factor in her marriage. A factor that's frequently overlooked and underrated. I brought up the subject with my own father, who promptly dismissed the bride's disappointment with a peremptory 'Nonsense.'

Why nonsense? The person you decide to share a substantial part of your life with, has to be someone who makes your heart race—at least in the first few years. That's not asking for too much. In fact, I'd consider it a basic, minimum requirement. Perhaps men have a different take on this, perhaps they label the condition differently. But it has to work for both. If there is zero passion, then there's zero romance.

Cynics often say that this sort of heart-pounding excitement is a teenage myth, a juvenile expectation. That girls who base their decision on mere physical attraction, end up marrying unworthy rakes who betray them.

Passion does not recognize age; it is certainly not reserved exclusively for teenagers. Ask M.F. Husain, if you don't believe me!

Similarly, men who marry overtly sexual women are asking for trouble. I abhor this theory. And completely understand the young bride's predicament: she likes her husband; she's not in love with him; and she definitely doesn't enjoy having sex with him—yet.

I told her, sexual compatibility can come later. In fact, in a healthy, loving relationship, the sexual equation only gets better, since the partners are better attuned to each other's needs. She didn't seem convinced! 'It's either there, or it's not there,' she said morosely.

My question to experts is: can it be created? Does it come later? Does familiarity breed only contempt? Or can it lead to a certain sexual charge too? My gut feeling tells me what the young bride already knows—either you have it or you don't. Sparks either fly, or they don't. You can't wish them to and then wait for the fire that never gets lit.

The next question, of course, is: how long does this

so-called passion last? Is passion alone enough to keep an otherwise 'good' marriage going? Difficult question. There are those who thrive on passion, or, at any rate, the heady idea of it. These sort of people cannot imagine a life devoid of that all-important 'frisson'. Once they experience it, even in a relationship that goes nowhere eventually, it's the single most important attribute they seek all through their lives. I recall a conversation with one of my young daughters while we were vacationing in Greece. She was between relationships and feeling somewhat lost and rudderless.

'If you miss the guy so much, why did you break off with him?' I asked bluntly. 'Of course I miss him,' she said, 'but he didn't do anything for me—ever! I liked him, sure, we had some super times together. But when I was with him, I used to keep thinking of other people I'd been attracted to and wondering why I wasn't feeling the same way about him. I felt disloyal even though I wasn't actually doing anything . . .'

I tried to give her the example of one of her girlfriends who'd married a real rake, only because he 'did something' to her. There she was, this trusting girl, slaving away for a man who routinely cheated on her. She endured that and more in silence, since it was she who had picked him, much to her family's distress. 'How far is this attraction going to take her?' I asked. My daughter smiled. 'Who knows? But at least she had the guts to go for the man who appealed to her . . .'

I thought then about M.F. Husain's fixation. Surely, there have been other, far lovelier actresses than Madhuri. He has known so many himself. And yet, it was Madhuri who enraptured him, took over his being completely. Who can explain this sort of an attraction? Question it? Challenge it? Pronounce judgement? Say it's wrong/right/foolish? Nobody. So it is with the dhak-dhak factor in marriage. There are those who make decisions with their heart, others with their head. Still others who lay more emphasis on the music made by two bodies in harmony. I, for one, never underestimate the role of physical attraction in a relationship. To those who scoff, I sternly say, 'Don't knock it, buddy, you have no idea how crucial it is.'

I am convinced you cannot have bodies-in-sync unless minds are in sync, too. The ideal situation is one where the partners actively appreciate and enjoy their physical togetherness. With love and trust, this bond can only get better, provided the foundation has been built on mutual attraction in the first place. In the old days, one really over-used word to describe this condition used to be 'chemistry'. I, for one, am a great believer in chemistry.

Even between people who are just friends (no sexual vibes), it is chemistry that cements the relationship. To those who wonder at what point this chemistry turns into an emotional acid-attack, I can only say, 'Pray that it doesn't happen to you.' I've been fortunate enough to know couples who have been together for twenty-five years and more, and for whom the sparks continue to fly. Genuinely so. They've never looked beyond their mates and are entirely satisfied with the equation. Today's generation might call this 'weird' or 'freaky', but in some odd way, I suspect these new kids on the block are actually envious! Incredulous and envious. They can't believe it's possible to stay resolutely in a relationship without straying or lusting after another.

There is a 'sensible' approach to handling the 'dhak-dhak' issue, and an irrational one. Most marriages collapse when the irrational outpaces the sensible. But there are those who prefer living in the appealingly crazy, borderline and 'irrational' zone and paying the high price for decisions taken at that level. Why not? Without the all-important 'dhak-dhak', there would be no great art or music or poetry. All creativity arises out of a primal 'dhak-dhak'. It is a driving force that knows no boundaries. The world's most inspiring love stories are based on 'dhak-dhak' (Romeo-Juliet, Heer-Ranjha, Laila-Majnu). Those who fear it, fear themselves. And eventually lose out on experiencing life's incomparable *joie de vivre* in all its richness.

Alas, most of our life stories are not scripted by Shakespeare. Many of us have to make do, carry on, smile, pretend and pose. No matter. For every human being there is at least one amazing, unforgettable, life-transforming 'dhak-dhak' moment. Recognize it. Cherish it. Relive it, if you can. It may never come back. And what an immense loss that would be! A passionless existence is just that—existence. Surely you deserve more?

- ♥ Dhak-dhak is a powerful, positive, persuasive emotion that drives any passionate relationship.
- ♥ Dhak-dhak, if missing in marriage, can lead to indifference and listlessness.
- ♥ It can leave partners exhausted and frustrated if their respective dhak-dhaks don't match or are not reserved for one another.
- ♥ Dhak-dhak goes well beyond vague lusting, and is far more all-encompassing. And yes, you can work at it!

Sixteen
Sex and the City
Tan man ka milan

Blame it on the city. Go on . . . you've found the perfect escape route. A hard-to-challenge alibi. The city is awful. It induces stress. There's no time. God, how tiring life has become. The pollution levels sap all energy. How can anyone think of sex with all that noise? Where's the privacy? The neighbours practically live in your pocket. After commuting forever, all you can think of is cuddling your pillow.

Great sex needs great commitment—where do you find that rare and precious commodity in this ghastly urban jungle? Weekend sex? Yes, sounds like a good idea—but what about the kids' cricket camp, weekly grocery shopping, parties, pedicures, in-law's visits, doctor's appointments, laundry, spring-cleaning, dog grooming, movies? Come on, with so much on the plate, who has the time for sex?

If any or all of this sounds familiar, drop whatever you are doing and give your marital sex-life serious thought. Do you enjoy sex with your partner? Do you participate actively, eagerly? Do you look forward to it? Does it matter to you whether or not you have it? Do you track the frequency and worry about declining statistics? Are you comfortable enough with your partner to discuss your feelings on the subject? Has sex become just another marital duty to be performed with the sort of regularity you keep for dental check-ups? If any of this sounds a bit too close to the truth, then a review is overdue. Don't blame the city. Blame yourself. Of course urban life isn't easy. And of course you fight everyday to stay on top of things. But if sex has become a low-priority area in your crowded life, it's time to take stock and reorganize a few things.

Make no mistake about it—sexual compatibility is perhaps the strongest, most enduring bond in any marriage. Most times it gets undervalued, only because the subject of sex itself is so threatening. Couples rarely 'discuss' sex— they just have it. I believe it's important to articulate how you feel about this very delicate, yet powerful area of your life together. If you are not in sync in this zone, chances are the incompatibility will colour several other areas without your even knowing it.

Couples who are too embarrassed or too indifferent to address their sexual drives do themselves a disservice. Far more than anything else, what eventually contributes to a good sexual equation is nothing more complex than achieving a comfortable level in your conversations on the subject. If you can break through your inhibitions on a verbal level, chances are you'll do the same on the physical level. Being uptight or oblique will get you nowhere. Sex demands a certain forthrightness, and what is a relationship worth if it cannot accommodate that?

Good communication is the basis of good sex. These days, couples look for ready excuses to avoid sex. Eventually, this leads to fatigue and boredom, ending in alienation and isolation. Partners who cannot articulate their sexual needs, out of fear that they'll be rejected or mocked, will withdraw completely or seek fulfilment elsewhere. The 'elsewhere' need not be another relationship; a rejected or humiliated partner is unlikely to jump into bed with the first available person. But certainly, a distancing will take place. Distancing that could end in divorce, or at any rate, desolation within marriage.

There is a great deal of ignorance about sex, even in this day and age. Even in urban India. Even with all the sex talk on TV and in our movies. Even with the new 'openness', it's amazing how little people actually know about their own bodies and the potential inherent in exploring physical avenues as a couple. Sometimes, I get asked the most astonishingly naïve questions by people I expect to be better informed. A lot of these queries emerge from a basic lack of understanding. And, I'm sorry to say, from distorted media projections.

> *If you don't feel good about yourself, you can't make your partner feel good either. Work on your self-esteem and confidence, and see the difference.*

Misrepresentation of modern sexual 'trends' can lead to confusion. Couples who feel they aren't hip enough because they don't experiment enough, get bogged down and discouraged. 'Threesomes are supposed to be "in", but I'm not ready for such stuff,' I heard a young wife say. Or, 'Our friends go to Bangkok for sandwich massages and group sex—are we prudes because we don't find this cool?' Or, 'My husband watches foreign porn films constantly, and thinks it's okay to demand kinky sex from me. If I refuse, he threatens he'll look for it somewhere else.' Or, 'My wife's girlfriends tell her she's leading a boring sex life. She wants to blindfold and whip me. Sorry . . . but that sort of thing turns me off.' Or, 'Is it normal for straight couples to have only anal sex?' Or, 'My husband says if he's having relationships with men, that isn't counted as being unfaithful. He says adultery is restricted to bedding another woman—is he fooling me?' Or, 'I'm constantly being criticized for not being adventurous in bed. When I ask what that means, I'm told to shut up and use my imagination.' Or, 'Sex is so overrated. People keep talking about it, but frankly, it's a big headache.' Or, 'Sex is a one-way street these days. All my partner cares about is his own pleasure.'

Maybe in that last 'accusation' lies the key. Sex, in a good marriage, is not about taking, but giving. It isn't about performance, it's about mutual pleasure. A man who's only focused on being a 'tiger in bed' can never be a sensitive lover to his wife who, poor creature, may not be a tigress in heat herself. Sexual compatibility is achieved over a period of time, and only through trust and caring.

Then, of course, there is the basic question of sex drive—if one of the partners happens to be a sexual demon with a high sex drive as compared to the other, who may not be able to keep up ('Three times a night—ten times a week? Ridiculous!'), it's a genuine problem requiring adjustment and accommodation from both. This, perhaps, is the single most frustrating sexual issue in marriage— how often? And who decides?

Women claim it's almost always the man who takes the

call. 'Why should sex be exclusively on his terms?' they ask. Quite rightly, too. But the men argue, 'Of course it's on our terms, we are the ones who have to get it up and get on with the job.' Women, who are increasingly setting the sexual pace in relationships and taking the initiative, have no use for these 'dumb' excuses. 'We want to be able to drive the sex-thing, too. What happens when I'm in the mood, and he is "thanda"? Do I just wait for him to get aroused—which could happen a week later? Or do I actively work on him?'

Women who 'actively work on' getting their partners to toe the sexual line, admit that the challenge is worth it. 'I feel less passive and more empowered, this way. After all, if I can make the effort to oblige him when I'd rather be watching TV, he can do likewise.' In all this struggle to achieve sexual equality in the bedroom, something very vital gives—romance and tenderness. You can't achieve sexual harmony by maintaining a score-card and giving marks. You can't view sex as a shopping list with 'must buys' that have to be ticked off.

Alas, too many couples, reading too many sex manuals, watching too many sex flicks and comparing too many (fake) notes on the subject, are discovering to their dismay that sex as an organized activity completely kills the libido. You can't pencil in 'sex time' for yourself like you pencil in 'treadmill: fifty minutes,' 'yoga: twenty minutes,' 'Buddhist chanting:

thirty minutes.' There is something called spontaneity, something known as the 'thrill' of sex. If sex is viewed as a 'project' or is 'result driven', that's the end. Couples who click best in this area are those whose attitude to sex is healthy and positive. If both partners view sexual activity in the same way, chances are they'll be able to work out the hiccups early on in marriage.

The biggest turn-offs in sex are ego and inhibition. Ego stops you from surrendering to your partner in a loving way. And it comes in the way of an honest expression of needs and feelings. Self-consciousness and fear form the two components of inhibition. These are more difficult to deal with since years of conditioning have gone into creating them. Young brides from conservative families are still raised to think of sex as something 'dirty' they have to comply with, in order to keep their husbands 'satisfied'. The question of their own satisfaction does not arise. If sex itself is projected as 'dirty', the husband who 'needs' it is seen as 'dirty' too. Especially in arranged marriages where the young bride is often completely in the dark about the birds and the bees and what actually happens in the marital boudoir on D-Day. Fed with half-truths and myths, the poor girl is scared and ignorant, and that's how she remains, unless the husband is sensitive or informed enough to handle her fears patiently and lovingly.

Today's young marrieds are caught in a peculiar time

warp. They receive mixed signals from their elders, and entirely confusing ones from peers. Sure, a lot of them have already sampled sex before marriage, but I'm still surprised by their levels of 'not knowing'. Contemporary culture tells them it's okay to indulge in whatever it takes to make sex exciting. And so they experiment wildly and irresponsibly, with everything from recreational drugs and multiple partners, to sex toys and assorted variants. Not all of them necessarily enjoy this adventure, since they cannot totally ignore the more conservative messages sent out by their folks—the older generation that still conforms to more conventional standards. As one young man said to me, 'I'm so mixed up. I've tried it all. And I'm still not sure what I really want from my partner . . . from sex . . . from marriage.'

Then there's the on-going Big 'O' debate with no resolution. Wives who crib that they never or rarely climax during intercourse have a point. While men who ask, 'How the hell are we supposed to guess whether or not the Big "O" has occurred?' also have a point. Women must speak up and voice their needs. It's only through dialogue of the non-accusatory kind that a breakthrough is possible. Sex, being such a highly sensitive issue, needs careful decoding. Words must be chosen with immense care, for they can have an awesome effect on sex. Used well, they act as an aphrodisiac, but used carelessly, they are serious inhibitors.

Think before you raise sexual issues with your partner. One cruel, insensitive put-down could cost you your sex life. It's true. So many couples have narrated incidents of unfortunate bedroom conduct that has effectively ruined intimacy forever.

This may surprise you, but thousands of Indian couples claim never to have seen their partners entirely naked. 'It is not necessary,' a woman once told me primly and rather angrily. 'What's the point? Where's the need? I'd rather not see, nor do I want to be seen. What for? You finish off the business quickly, and that's it.' She'd hit the nail on the head. Sex is seen as a 'business' to be conducted in the dark and as fast as possible. Sex is also seen as nothing more than a

Remember, sex is often in the head. Do not mock, criticize or rate a 'performance'. Sex is not a challenge with a trophy at the end.

procreational activity or a periodic (mainly male) need that needs to be fulfilled. The question of getting to know (and like!) one another's bodies remains unimportant. As the lady asked, 'What for?'

Modern marriages aren't doing much better, alas. After the first few years, sex becomes functional, a 'duty fuck' with very little emotional investment. Couples go through the motions mechanically, without bothering with niceties like ambience, mood, or even a readiness for physical intimacy. 'Sometimes, we do it with the TV blaring. My husband's attention is on cricket scores or something on the news. We rarely undress. My mind is on domestic matters—whether the tadka has been given properly to the daal. There's nothing romantic about our love-making.' When I say there can be, most couples laugh!

'Forget romance-shomance. Where's the time for all that—we can barely manage sex, with all the load we have taken on. We worry, worry, worry constantly. Car loan, house loan, credit card bills, tuition fees, travel expenses. God! The last thing on my mind is romance. Sex is okay. We all need sex. But forget the frills!'

I want to scream, 'It's the frills that count, stupid! Ignore the frills and what you're doing is copulating, not making love. Discover the difference.'

The biggest challenge in most Indian families is to deal with numbers—the joint family is perhaps the equivalent of a really, really cold shower for an amorous couple in search of romantic sex. How the hell does one create an appropriate mood, with assorted in-laws milling around a restricted space? Kids may indulge in persistent knocking, right when the big moment is imminent. Aunts, uncles, visitors may be right across the paper-thin wall separating your room from the hall. Nights in white satin? Candles? Lounge music? Fragrant oils? Chocolates? Forget it. These are fantasies for most couples looking for that stolen hour in which to get transported to another plane. Aaah, we've got the right word. We've hit it! Fantasy! When reality intrudes and inhibits you from living out your sexual adventures, you can always fall back on fantasy.

It's a matter of training your brain, your imagination. It's not just possible, it's worth doing. It's not such a tough technique, once you get the hang of it. Focus your mind on any image you find sexually arousing—no taboos, no restrictions. Concentrate on that image while shutting out your actual environment. Once you get the mental picture you most enjoy, the rest is easy. But for it to work, you need to know your own body as well as your partner's. Unless the two bodies are 'friends', they cannot be in sync.

It's equally important to set time aside—not as in 'Let's pencil in sex for Wednesday night between 10.30 and 11 . . . that's providing we don't go out, or my meeting doesn't get extended,' but as something you both look forward to. A mutually desirable activity that isn't linked to any other.

Marital sex is known as the world's greatest stress-buster. Apart from several health benefits, it has been established that couples who maintain physical intimacy over years are generally better adjusted and happier all around. Besides, sexologists will tell you, sex can only get better with time, if your attitude is right. Don't let humdrum routine and boredom ruin your loving. Recognize the importance of sex in your marriage. Never underrate or take that aspect of your married life for granted. Stay in tune with your partner, mentally and emotionally. Only then can sex become an exciting, enjoyable, pleasurable, fulfilling journey.

To keep the sexual magic going . . .

♥ Good communication is the first step towards good sex. If you cannot tell your partner about your likes, dislikes, turn-ons, turn-offs, how on earth will you achieve sexual compatibility?

♥ Personal hygiene is crucial when it comes to intimacy. Make sure you are showered and 'nice smelling' before getting into bed. If you can't shower, at least use a good deo. Nothing kills sex more effectively than b.o. and bad breath.

♥ A pleasant ambience goes a long way. Even if you don't get into creating an elaborate setting, it's worth tidying up the room, adjusting the lighting and—most importantly—switching off the bloody TV!

♥ Carve out time for physical closeness. It need not lead to sex, but it's important to maintain close body, mind and soul contact.

♥ A good meal plays a role in good sex. Even the anticipation of one gets the juices going. It's difficult to enjoy sex if one or both are on a starvation diet—all you'll be thinking of, in that case, is food, not foreplay.

♥ Relax and enjoy your moments of sexual togetherness. Showering together is a lovely prelude, as is a light massage.

♥ Sex should never be about scoring points and settling scores. Women tend to use sex as a weapon or a reward, withdrawing when they want to make a point. This is childish and hurtful. Domestic issues should be dealt with separately, across a table, not in bed.

♥ You can't harass your partner for sex. It negates the purpose.

♥ If you see yourself heading towards a sexual, physical, or emotional burn-out, take some time off with your partner. Unwind, chill out, rediscover your own potential in a new, stress-free environment.

♥ Couples with very young kids often find themselves too exhausted to make time for sex (daunting prospect, with bawling brats and hyper-energetic toddlers). Grab whatever time and privacy you possibly can, and laugh over your predicament—it's not going to last forever.

♥ When all else fails, turn to fantasy. An over-heated sexual imagination has saved many a dull marriage. There's nothing like vivid imagery to put the zing back into your sex life.

♥ Don't take sex or your partner so much for granted that you reduce both to mechanical devices.

♥ Be bold and fearless while expressing your sexual preferences. Don't blame your partner if he or she does not press the right buttons—it won't happen if you don't talk.

♥ Do something you consider 'wicked' at least once in your life. Not only will it spice up the monotony of your marital life if it has fallen into a rut, it will make you feel great!

Seventeen
Sex It Up, Baby!
Kuch love, kuch masti

A few months ago I attended a hi-voltage, really, really splashy wedding of a sweet and harmless young man I'd watched growing up with my kids. He seemed deliriously happy with his bride of a few hours. Over dinner, I got talking to his school friends, most of whom were still single. 'Marriage is a dumb option,' one of the young men said. 'Look at this poor sucker with that foolish grin on his face. Two years from now, he'll be crying.'

What a cynical observation, I said to the boy, who shrugged. 'Unless I meet a woman who I believe can keep the excitement levels up well after we're married, I won't bother with marriage at all. At the end of a year or so, it becomes so boring, so predictable.'

Excitement? Hmmm, why not? But what sort of excitement? 'Well, I like watching soft porn . . . I guess, most guys my age do. I would find it sexually stimulating to watch it with my partner, without embarrassment or shame. If my wife is uncomfortable about this, then sorry, it wouldn't work.'

Similar views were expressed by both sexes in that age bracket (25-30). The women wanted 'freedom and variety' in their marriage, meaning they wanted to experiment with casual relationships and holiday flings, without being made answerable. 'How does it matter? Such "affairs" have no bearing on our permanent relationship. They don't count. If anything, they spice up a marriage.'

There were girls who said they wanted to extend their sexual landscape within marriage to include multiple partners, same-sex love, threesomes and gadgets. 'There's nothing wrong with experimentation. Life becomes so dull with just one partner whose moves you know. Our generation seeks novelty and thrills. It could be anything— a stripper at home or an erotic mujra party. It could be a rain dance, or a wild dunking party at Holi . . . these things sometimes lead to more masti. So long as your partner knows and is okay with it, where's the problem?'

The more I interact with young unmarrieds (and a few

marrieds), I realize how far they've come in terms of what is acceptable and unacceptable in marriage. 'Fidelity is over-rated,' they say nonchalantly. 'It's masala that makes a marriage buzz. These days you need to spice up stale relationships with something more than candles and wine.'

Well, I agree with one part of this argument, and that is the part that deals with 'spicing up' a marriage. But there are countless less rash ways of doing that. For example, a well-timed massage always but always succeeds in pressing the right button. There's nothing more relaxing, or potentially arousing, than a massage given by an attentive partner. And these days, with the easy availability of wonderfully fragrant aroma therapy oils, even a half-hour weekly massage can transform the quality of your marital life. Given the stress levels all urban creatures deal with on a daily basis, it's worth it to carve out those crucial thirty minutes just to relax, touch, smell and surrender. Aromatic candles heighten the experience, as does soothing music.

But for all of this to actually work, the mind has to be receptive. Couples who find the exercise 'silly' or 'wasteful' will never be able to enjoy the simple pleasure of a back rub or a neck massage. Why, the fairly easy task of pressing your partner's feet and pulling the toes gently till they crack can be accomplished even in the backseat of a car. Try it.

The Truth About Marriage

'I like a little wickedness in my marriage,' a stodgy banker once confessed, much to everybody's shock and astonishment. His wife smiled indulgently but revealed nothing. The other men teased the banker and asked him to expand on what he meant by 'wicked'. 'Well,' said the guy, without a trace of embarrassment, 'I like to come home and find a stark naked wife waiting in bed for me. I like the unexpected, the whimsical. I like fantasy, because the rest of my life is so businesslike and prosaic.'

Marital routines are unavoidable. But it helps to break them occasionally and do something unpredictable and unexpected.

The man had found his match in his wife, who obviously went along with his little games and tricks. 'There's nothing kinky about our relationship,' he added hastily, 'but we feel completely comfortable with each other and that means we feel completely confident too.' Confidence is the key. The man had identified the one quality that is needed in any sexual exchange for it to be complete.

'What's kinky, anyway?' people frequently ask. 'Who decides what's odd and what's not?' This is true. So long as the people involved are not imposing their hang-ups on anyone else, it's fine. I think of Stanley Kubrick's controversial film *Eyes Wide Shut*, which explored the darker, more secret side of a husband's sexuality, which eventually leads to the couple confronting their true selves. It was an intriguing film which raised several questions and few answers. But it allowed, rather it persuaded viewers to examine their own suppressed sexual emotions if they dared.

'Masala' comes with its own connotations. I've met young couples who get their kicks from speed, danger, drugs, alcohol, abuse, S&M rituals, blindfolds—oh, the whole gamut of artificial aids and contraptions. I believe if a marriage becomes overdependent on stimulants of any kind, it actually displays its inherent structural faults. Couples who get addicted to pornography, or are in search of sexual innovation in a compulsive way, are, in fact, in some sort of denial about their own impulses. Young men who can't keep away from call girls, or who spend inordinate amounts of time in chatrooms that encourage sex talk, and women who're hooked to phone sex with strangers, or who routinely exchange provocative SMSs with men not their partners, definitely need to ask themselves a few questions.

I heard a young man saying with genuine surprise in his voice, 'I don't know what her problem is . . . I've been totally faithful . . . hookers don't count . . . that's just fooling around when she isn't here.' When asked whether identical standards would apply in the case of his wife, he was shocked. 'Certainly not! She's my wife . . . no way. How dare you suggest something like that? My wife isn't one of those chaalu women who sleeps around. I'd divorce her if she ever fooled around with another man.'

Many wives argue that a lesbian relationship does not amount to infidelity, since no penetration is involved. 'It's only fondling . . . that's nothing. Besides, it's not another man—it's a woman who's a good friend. Why should my husband mind? It's so harmless.' But the same wife is horrified at the thought of her husband indulging in a gay encounter. 'That's not on. It's sick!' How so?

Jealousy and casual flirtation are two of the most common areas of conflict among young couples. Both can be potentially destructive. 'Sometimes I enjoy watching my wife dance with other guys,' said a youngish husband. 'So long as I know it stops there, it's a sexy visual. Yes, I do feel a little jealous. But it's healthy jealousy that acts as a trigger in our relationship and keeps me on my toes. It makes me aware that my wife is attractive to other guys, and that if I don't watch out, I could lose her. It also shows that I'm not the only man to desire her. That makes her doubly attractive to me. I'm sure she feels the same when she sees me buying drinks for other chicks, or paying them attention. It's fun, within limits. We discuss it frankly, and it's not an issue.'

Sometimes I wonder if these young couples aren't

watching too much American television. Is this really what they believe keeps their marriage alive—bar flirtations and pole dancing with strangers? If so, their marriages will go the way they do in sit-coms—without the canned laughter, too.

To get the zing-thing going in marriage, the one important ingredient is interest. If your partner interests you enough, you instinctively know how and when to press the right buttons. Just the other day, the owner of a travel agency told us about a couple who had celebrated their wedding anniversary atop a glacier. They wanted it all— candlelight, a gourmet meal, music and complete privacy. He was glad to oblige (for a fat fee, of course!). He mentioned how romantically adventurous young Indians were getting these days, but even with his reassurances and endorsements, I couldn't help thinking it's a generation of culturally lost people looking for a quick fix in marriage in exactly the same way they seek quick fixes in other areas of their lives.

Movies and their absurd interpretations of love, for instance, affect attitudes in a way I find comical. A lot of the masala being mixed into the marriage pot-pourri takes its cues from popular cinema. Couples who seek to find their own formula are less likely to feel disappointed when violins don't soar each time they kiss.

Sexual games can tease and tantalize the imagination up

to a point, but how many different ways are there to give a back rub? Or should one ask Mick Jagger?

The key is to make your partner feel special, and if an unexpected, unscheduled gesture or gift can achieve that, it's worth investing in. Anniversaries and birthdays must never be ignored—never. They provide at least two wonderful reasons to do something out of the ordinary together. I remember any number of exciting unplanned developments that made our special days really, really special. Agreed, my husband is a great romantic, but mere romantic thoughts are not enough. To take those further, you need planning and imagination.

An anniversary weekend in, say, Goa, can become memorable, if it includes small, personalized touches, such as encouraging your partner to pack his favourite CDs/ wine/food or secretely buying a sexy negligee/sarong/ swimsuit just for the trip. No woman can resist flowers— even a few strings of fragrant gajra purchased at a traffic light can instantly lift the mood and lead to a mellow, magical evening. As can a changed table setting with a few culinary flourishes. The idea is to do something out of the ordinary, something eccentric and unpredictable, that charms the partner without necessarily overwhelming the senses. Luxury cruises have their devotees. I know a cruise-addict couple who can't get enough of the seven seas. They've taken every available cruise—Mediterranean,

Caribbean, Alaskan—and discovered something new about each other on each trip!

Spa weekends are rapidly gaining in popularity. I know a besotted young husband who 'gifted' a super-relaxing spa weekend to his beautiful wife, with some of the spa's most expensive treatments, including a caviar facial! No occasion, no agenda, no strings. Just his way of saying 'You deserve the extra pampering—enjoy it.'

There are wives who knit pullovers and husbands who buy 'no strings attached' gifts. There are couples who specialize in erotic SMSs or e-mails that need serious censorship. There are even those who stage elaborate costume parties for each other—a husband who likes to see his wife performing a private striptease or a tantalizing mujra. Or a wife who loves rain dancing at their beach bungalow and says the best part is when she gets to remove his soaking wet clothes! Some men sing, others compose couplets, still others focus on exotic food, chocolates and wine. But, say the experts, the most fun young couples have is at the gym, sweating it out first and

Watch out for those 'harmless' flirtations—they have a nasty way of backfiring, especially if they occur on a holiday and follow you back to your home.

then chilling in a jacuzzi.

A lot of energetic newly-marrieds insist they like the idea of unprogrammed sexual interludes. Such as in the morning, just before leaving for work. The thought that it could disrupt schedules and throw things out of gear becomes a turn-on. 'It's worth the inconvenience . . . missed appointments, screwed-up schedules. What the hell! If you can't bluff your way out with the boss, all you are is a worker ant.'

Timing is everything. And so is the location. Couples who use all the areas of their home for love-making insist that's what keeps the passion on a boil. Bedrooms are always there. And so are biweekly, pre-bedtime couplings. But those who boldly venture into the living room mid-afternoon, or check out the erotic possibilities of a shower stall, gloat that these little deviations from the routine add a lot of energy to their sex lives.

In other words . . .

- ♥ Sex should never be equated with 'duty' or a domestic chore ('Oh God . . . today is Thursday—dhobi day, as well as sex before dinner').
- ♥ Pep up your sex life with whatever it takes to keep it alive and interesting.
- ♥ If you have to trot out an excuse, make it more original than 'Not tonight, I have a headache.'

- Masala needs to be added judiciously. Too much of it can kill the subtlety of the moment, too little can lead to blandness.

- Weekends off need not have a fixed agenda—must wash the car, sort out tax matters, visit in-laws, fix the phone, get new curtains, speak to investment banker, have sex in the afternoon. Keep them flexible and see how much fun that is.

- Holidays must never fall into a pattern—in fact, few things should. Take off during the week, leave kids with accommodating in-laws, or understanding friends. Take a few ummm . . . errr . . . unusual DVDs along if that's your kick. The important thing is to switch off . . . relax . . . enjoy each other.

- Changing your appearance radically is an easy option and worth trying, if you are adventurous enough to do so. It breaks the monotony of waking up next to the same old face, year in and year out..

- Imagination is your best tool—use it!!

Eighteen
One-night Stands
Raat baaki, baat baaki

'Big deal'. Those are the two words that invariably accompany any discussion on the subject of this potentially dangerous-to-a-relationship subject. Today's more liberal generation takes it for granted that partners will stray. 'As long as it isn't serious,' they hastily clarify, when asked.

I find this argument shaky. Who decides how serious? What is the yardstick used? Do both partners sit down and define what 'serious' means? What if they don't agree? Assuming it really is a silly fling for one, does the other have the right to object and say, 'Sorry, but I don't find it silly. I am deeply hurt'? Does a 'one-night stand' fall into a separate, special category? Is it taken as a lesser evil—not a full-blown case of infidelity, but just a mild, temporary infection, no more serious than a superficial rash that generally disappears when ignored?

'Infidelity is major,' an earnest young banker explained to me. 'Infidelity can wreck a marriage, and often does. But a one-night stand? Come on . . . get real . . . everybody has one at some time or the other. It doesn't mean a thing.' I asked bluntly whether his wife was aware of his views. He said jauntily, 'Of course . . . we talk about it often.'

Talking was one thing. Had he indulged in a one-night stand himself? He looked over his shoulder to check that his wife wasn't within earshot and smiled slyly. 'You know the answer to that one.' As a matter of fact, I did. I happened to know his 'fling', and she was far from amused. In fact, she'd been devastated to discover that was how he thought of her. And she wasn't about to go away quietly. I told him so. He looked a little startled, but not terribly concerned. 'Women!' he said, 'stupid cows! What was she thinking? She'd had a few shots too many. I'd had a few myself. My wife was out of town . . . and you know . . . things happened. Does that mean I have to marry the bitch now?'

I found his attitude offensive, but also predictable. Most men would feel the same way. And clarify that the woman they'd bedded so casually was not underage, nor had any force been applied. 'As an aware, consenting adult, she ought to have known what she was getting into. If she didn't, too bad for her!' is how the banker put it. On one level (the rational), he was absolutely right. On another (the emotional), his thinking was gross and caddish. This is precisely what makes this whole business of one-night stands so tricky. The terrain is ambiguous, the rules of the game ill-defined.

Two can play the cheating game. Are you ready to accept or overlook your partner's fling?

In earlier times, men with opportunities and means thought sexual dalliance was a perfectly acceptable form of social intercourse. Especially if the women they picked happened to be foreigners, or worse, sex-workers. 'It has nothing to do with my marriage or my wife,' I've heard countless men claim, rather disingenuously—unless, of course, I've got it all wrong. Perhaps they were really and truly convinced about the validity of cheating on their partners, provided the 'cheating' was restricted to one night at a time. Even after it became a pattern in their marriage, it was still treated as an entirely unimportant, casual issue— regardless of what the wife may feel about it.

A lot of women I spoke to evaded the subject and seemed uncomfortable discussing their husband's indiscretions. Some were candid (or resigned) enough to say, 'What can we do about it even if we know? It's too late to leave and start all over again.' The question of dealing with hurt and pain was never answered. It was as if they'd bought a package when they married, and accepted the downside with a philosophical shrug. A few admitted it often worked both ways—they had their own distractions on the side, and the marriage remained undamaged and undented through all these liaisons. I find that difficult to swallow. I have yet to meet anyone—even the most liberal/liberated person, who is completely unfazed by infidelity. Even the world's most debauched husbands would feel betrayed and outraged if their wives had affairs.

In our society, affairs have been conveniently dubbed as 'elitist pursuits' indulged in by decadent urban millionaires. This is a completely misleading premise. One only has to look at newspaper reports to see the staggering number of crimes committed by jealous spouses or paramours. Even middle-class India is not spared, no matter what the popular perception. This shift is evident in the way infidelity has become the leitmotif of our TV soaps and the staple of popular Hindi films. In the south, the old tradition of maintaining a 'little wife' continues in a new garb. But it is very much a reality, with modern packaging, of course.

One-night stands are potentially dangerous to any relationship that aims for permanence and security. They simply do not work, for the elementary reason that such irresponsible encounters seriously erode trust. And with trust taken out of the equation, there's little hope for love to survive.

Recently, I was pleasantly surprised when one of my sons said, 'I'm finally ready to handle a regular relationship, a traditional one—no games, no fooling around.' He must have seen the surprised look on my face, for he hastily assured me that he'd given a lot of thought to it and come to the conclusion that a relationship can only work when the two people involved are one hundred per cent honest with each other. And that honesty did not mean confessing to the partner that yes, there had been a few 'mistakes' along the way. Couples who imagine a confessional takes care of all the guilt and solves problems, are only deluding themselves. More often than not, these sort of whiney talkathons lead to bitterness and worse complications. Nothing is really resolved, nothing achieved.

Besides, one-night stands have a nasty way of backfiring on participants. You never know when a casual quickie in a broom-closet can lead to international headlines (if you are Boris Becker), a paternity suit (ditto) and a love-child requiring life-time support (ditto, ditto). Even if you aren't Boris Becker, what with sophisticated DNA-testing, it's impossible to shrug off responsibility and go scot-free, if the partner decides to follow through and nail the offender.

Casual sex has its adherents. There are those who insist it helps perk up a marriage that may have fallen into a rut.

It's considered 'cool' to discuss multiple partners and hold forth on half-baked theories that suggest man was never made for monogamy. If you ask me, it's not about moral issues alone, it's also about health (mental, emotional, physical) in marriage. It's very difficult to accept the presence of another in a committed relationship. Even the world's most progressive, most liberal intellectuals who experimented with what was called 'free love', confessed later in life, that despite their public posturing and claims to the contrary, they did feel bitter and betrayed when they discovered their partner's infidelities.

The most famous couple in the literary world—Jean Paul Sartre and Simone de Beauvoir, who advocated a no-strings-attached relationship and never married, eventually admitted (at least, de Beauvoir did) that their long-term relationship was turbulent and rocky, mainly because of all the affairs they conducted outside the association. What was agreed upon in a cerebral context did not work on the emotional plane. Beauvoir wrote heart-breakingly about the pain she endured each time Sartre strayed. Is it worth it to subject oneself to such negativity?

A lot of young marrieds come up with the stale theory that 'What you don't know doesn't hurt.' I've heard husbands saying jauntily, 'As long as I'm discreet and she doesn't find out, what does it matter?' Wives, increasingly, are saying this, too. Middle-class India is obviously in the process of reassessing old values and trying on new roles.

Urban India is more mobile, more ambitious, more accepting of change. As a friend's married daughter put it, 'I never ask my husband what he's up to when he travels, either in India or abroad. Frankly, I'd rather not know. I also hate it if he cross-examines me and keeps track of my whereabouts in his absence. If he's having a good time in Dubai with someone he met at a party or in a bar, well, that's his life, his option. I don't want to know about it. We don't believe in the confessional form of marriage. When he comes back, I don't grill him. Neither does he ask me stupid questions like, "Where did you go? What did you do? Who did you meet?" It's understood between us. That's why we rarely fight.'

I was entirely convinced, till I met the same girl a couple of years later. She was divorced and looking ten years older. Familiar story: a romance that refused to die or go away. While her husband was on a business trip, she decided to 'date' an acquaintance, who didn't know he was meant to disappear on her husband's return. Meanwhile, the husband had also been 'dating' a colleague in London, each time he went there (five times a year). Now this couple was in a fix since neither wanted to break off the so-called 'casual' relationships. Accusations led to fights, which led to temporary separation, which ended in divorce. 'Our lifestyles finally caught up with us,' she said sadly. 'We realized we couldn't really cope with the silly cover-ups.'

Victims of this new morality can be found all over the world. It is the veterans who confuse and baffle me. Such as this middle-aged friend of ours who makes it a point to flash his 'girlfriends', while his ever-smiling wife pretends it's all a huge joke and that she loves her husband for being who he is—a large-hearted, outgoing flirt who adores young, good-looking companions. These two have been married for nearly thirty years. To all appearances, they're an extraordinarily well-adjusted couple. They have annoying pet names for each other, which they scrupulously stick to in public, and it isn't unusual to see them kissing and cooing at parties. 'We married young,' the wife

If there are no sparks left in your marriage and you can't do without casual affairs, why are you still in the marriage?

once told me, 'we were like kids ourselves. My husband didn't get the chance to have any girlfriends when boys his age were dating. Now, he wants to make up for lost opportunities. So what? I don't feel threatened or insecure.'

Maybe they have arrived at a stage where their love for each other really does extend well beyond possessiveness. The one question that remains unasked is whether this privilege is the husband's alone, as I suspect it must be. Is the wife 'allowed' to catch up on all the dates she could have enjoyed during her teenage years but didn't? I doubt it. In which case, it's a lopsided deal loaded in the man's favour. If it works, it's because she's resigned and maybe relieved too (his peccadilloes perhaps free her from her sexual obligations). I must ask her when we next meet.

Even with young adults, the problem of one-night-stands continues to be just that—a problem. Friends of my teenage daughters often spend hours at our home weeping over boyfriends who have been caught straying. I even know of a twelve-year-old whose heart was broken when she discovered her fourteen-year-old boyfriend had gone to the movies with a common friend and actually held hands with her! Despite the boy's protestations—'I only did it because she was scared, it was such a spooky film!'—the young girl refused to forgive him. 'I've broken off with him—he can't be trusted,' she announced solemnly, as schoolfriends called to console and sympathize.

What I noted was, not a single person 'condoned' the young boy's hand-holding. 'If he can do that now, he'll do worse things later,' they all agreed, as the little girl self-righteously wrote him a 'Dear John' letter announcing the end of their six-month-old relationship! Amusing? Sure. But telling, too. Chances are (and this is a wild guess), the little girl comes from a conservative home, with parents in a stable, positive relationship. This has been my observation all along—it's the message delivered by parents that strongly influences moral decisions, especially those that involve love, marriage, fidelity.

So, remember:

- ♥ One-night stands have a nasty way of backfiring. Think of broom closets and Boris Becker before you jump.
- ♥ How casual is casual? Who says casual can't get serious?
- ♥ Prepare yourself for the consequences. Is your marriage worth less than a night or two of indulgence?
- ♥ This may sound crazy, but in these strange times, one can't rule out blackmail if things sour.
- ♥ There's no such thing as a 'perfect secret'. Eventually, you'll get found out. Are you ready to face the music when you are?
- ♥ Gauging a partner's 'understanding' is not as easy as it appears. The same partner may turn around and accuse you of betrayal.
- ♥ One-nighters have a nasty way of adding up to big numbers. When that happens, and you're hooked to regular dalliance outside marriage, beware! It's a sure sign that there's trouble ahead. And it's called divorce.

Nineteen
Long-distance Love
Pardesi, pardesi, jaana nahin

I watched the disintegration of a long-distance marriage with a sense of sadness and some guilt. I'd seen it coming for over two years, and I'd kept quiet. In the old days, I would have spoken up and alerted my acquaintance. But that was in the old days. Watching this particular marriage fall apart, I'd said to myself, 'Who the hell are you to interfere? They haven't asked for your advice. It is none of your business. Besides, these are young people. They know what they're doing. It works differently these days.

Equations have changed. Stay out.'

That's what I did—stayed out. Till one day, the distraught husband broke down at my dining table and confessed it was all over. Yes, he loved his wife desperately. He loved his kid even more. But what was to be done? They'd drifted apart after five years of trying hard to keep the relationship going. Now, his wife had found a life without him. And he? Well, he'd taught himself to cope. It was time to move on for both of them. But that didn't mean he was relieved. Oh, no! The man was emotionally destroyed. He wanted his marriage back. Alas, it was too late.

This is becoming a familiar scenario, especially in our cities where the two-income family is here to stay. Both partners are committed careerists. Both are ambitious. Both travel. Both are absentee parents. Generally, there's one child. Sometimes, there's none. It's tough enough if they live in the same city and keep frenzied schedules. Imagine how much tougher it is when they live in two different cities, or worse, two entirely different time zones. My friend, the sad-eyed marketing whiz, was married to another marketing whiz. Between them they'd created an enviable 'lifestyle' which they valued. The kid was looked after by obliging in-laws and expensive nannies, while the two zipped around India and the world, attending conferences and seminars. They loved their respective jobs and loved each other. The man was supportive in every way and revelled in his wife's success. She was driven and focused on her next career goal—which was to head the division in her company. Well, she got the job all right. But not in the same city. It was in London. And she wanted it. Badly. Fine, said the sporting husband. No problem. Take it. I'll handle the kid. You go make a success of yourself.

After a round of farewell parties, the wife left to begin her new life, promising to visit once every three months. Great, said the husband, I'll hold the fort and bring the kid across during summer vacations. And yes, I'll try and time my own business trips to London to coincide with your breaks. Fantastic, said the wife, as she settled into her high-pressure job, secure in the knowledge that all was well on the domestic front. Sure, the kid cried a lot. And started bed-wetting. But the counsellors said it was normal. Just a phase. It will take a while, but this will pass.

It didn't. The kid was miserable. And so was the brave husband, whose life had been turned upside down with the new responsibility of playing mommy. The weekends, specially, were a nightmare, with kiddie activities and non-stop tantrums. All this for the additional income that was supposed to add 'quality' to their lives. Yes, he could afford a second car now, and buy that laptop. He'd planned a luxury cruise to Alaska in summer and invested in a holiday home. But God, was he unhappy! Most of the extra money and time went into long-distance phone calls. The wife was rarely available. And the kid got to talk to mom on the occasional Sunday when the time difference worked out in such a way that the conversation didn't clash with the kid's nap or meal time. It was bloody hard, but worth the sacrifice. Or so the adults thought. The kid would go to the best school. They'd make sure the best tutors were hired. The bank loan would get paid off. It was going to be a wonderful life for all.

That's not how it worked out. I really don't know what went wrong, the man said, weeping uncontrollably. We both tried our best. I was faithful to her. I know she was faithful to me. But somewhere, we lost our way. It was very difficult to maintain the same level of closeness. We were lonely and miserable most of the time. At least, I was. The kid was the loneliest of all, with a frequent change of irresponsible maids and a lack of continuity. Soon, the obsessive phone calls became less frequent. The guy felt he was intruding into his wife's space each time he phoned at a slightly 'awkward' hour and found her preoccupied. His work was suddenly not that important or interesting any more. He was drinking every evening—'Just to relax and stop myself from brooding.' The kid cried constantly and refused to be left alone even for a few hours at night. There was guilt, guilt and more guilt all around.

One day, the wife called and said she'd been offered a

better job—but this time in New York. It was a fantastic break and her rivals were most jealous. What did he think? Take it, he said. He meant it sincerely. Such opportunities were rare in the international career bazaar. Do you mean it? she asked in surprise. Of course, he said. Don't worry. I'll continue to handle the kid. Congratulations. We must celebrate. Errrrr . . . will you be coming to India before flying off? Ooops. Not likely to, she said a little sheepishly. I have to report on Monday, a week from now. There's lots to wrap up right here in London. Perhaps a couple of months from now? Okay, he said. No problem.

> *There is no substitute for togetherness— physical and emotional.*

That night he drank more than his usual quota of three stiff ones. He couldn't make it to work the next day. And he missed the kid's PTA. A persistent pain in the gut told him it was time to visit the family doc. Nervous exhaustion. Poor diet. Stress. Not enough sleep. Ulcer. If you don't watch it, buddy, you're dead. That's what the doc said.

Meanwhile, there was pressure at work, targets that hadn't been met and lots of travel. That left the big question: What to do with the poor kid? Boarding school? He was way too young for that. In-laws? Yes and no. Sympathetic friends? Well, as a short-term arrangement, maybe.

The man loved his wife. Admired her a lot, too. But if,

in the past, their time together was restricted to meeting at European airports between flights to different destinations, now even that contact was going to end with his wife flying across the Atlantic. He knew in his heart that the marriage was over. He felt wretched about his own life and, particularly, about his kid's life. Yes, he had strayed a couple of times out of sheer loneliness. He didn't know or even want to know whether his wife had done the same. The woman he dated off and on was like his wife—a woman in love with herself and her career. She'd made it clear she wasn't going to hang around baby-sitting both him and his kid. The man felt completely powerless, perhaps for the first time in his life.

There are thousands of young Indians like this couple. In Mumbai alone, I meet several. Either both individuals live on airplanes, or they operate out of different cities. Some insist they've hit upon a magic formula and joke that they really couldn't handle any more togetherness even if they tried. They like their own space (professional and personal) and are perfectly happy being solo most of the time. When they do synchronize schedules, it's great. And if their meetings are erratic and infrequent, it's pretty cool.

'We are not crippled without one another. We don't feel emotionally paralysed either. We've taught ourselves to negotiate and navigate quite expertly. There is very little dependence.'

Most of these marriages break up within five years. Some merrily, some not. The ones that opt for a friendly parting of ways generally fall into a comfortable long-term pattern, minus overt hostility or a show of acrimony. The reason is simple: ground rules have been worked out well in advance. Nothing much is at stake to begin with. Both earn. Both pay their own bills. Nothing is jointly owned. It works while it works. When the arrangement ceases to hold the interest of either one or both, the marriage is declared 'over'. They move on. Some remain buddies; most find other partners. Nothing actually changes in their individual lives. Nothing was meant to, in the first place.

I ask these people, why did they bother to get married? The answers vary, but the general explanation goes something like this: It sounded like a great idea at the time. We'd studied together, worked together. We knew each other's lives inside out. We always knew how important our respective careers were going to be. Life in two cities? Well, that's the risk one takes.

When I hear of such long-distance marriages, I am reminded of a conversation I had with a taxi driver in Dubai. There we were, driving back from a distant golf course, when the taxi driver spoke to me. 'From India?' he asked brightly. Once nationality was established, there was no stopping him. 'Ten years,' he said, shaking his head mournfully. 'I have been away from Kerala for ten long years. Money is good. But everything else, hopeless. I see my family once in two years for no more than forty days. When I go home, my children don't recognize me. Even my wife takes some time to adjust. I feel like a stranger. I feel they don't really need me—they only need my money.'

What a sad way to feel about yourself—as nothing more than a cheque that pays the bills. Poor man. I asked him why he didn't quit and go back—surely he'd made enough? 'What is enough?' he asked me. I had no answer.

His story is not unique. There are millions of husbands compelled by circumstances to live away from their wives and children. How do they cope? Can a marriage survive long separations? Well, in ancient times, men went to war. Some returned after years. Others weren't as lucky. In their absence, the womenfolk carried on, stoically. And waited, with a prayer on their lips and hope in their hearts. Today's women are different. Besides, today's women are travelling a great deal themselves, often spending as many hours, days or months away from home as their husbands. Obviously, they've worked out some sort of a system, which does not destroy their marriage—at least for a few years!

Certain professions demand long absences—Britons actually sympathized with Victoria Beckham when her husband, footballer David Beckham, was sold to Real Madrid and left for Spain. Corporate India is full of couples on the move. I can tell you, it isn't easy. Sure, families do get used to missing family members, but something always gives—generally, it's the emotional well-being of the partner who stays put. Anger and even envy set in at some point. ('Why the hell am I stuck in this dump, looking after the kids and pets while he or she traipses around the world having a blast?') Unless the person is an exceptionally generous, giving, caring individual.

Travelling couples also run the risk of drifting, out of a sense of isolation and loneliness in a new city. Occasionally, the initial excitement of being alone and free gets rapidly replaced by depression and martyrdom. ('I'm giving up so much for the sake of my family. Look at them, sitting comfortably in front of the TV or lolling around lazily while I slog in this foreign country, all by myself. What if I have a heart attack tonight? Will anyone know or care? All my family bothers about is how much money I send them.') It's a no-win situation for both, if you ask me. Like the poor cabbie who said he was stuck in the Middle East since his family was now accustomed to a certain standard of living and worse—his long absences! He said frankly that even he couldn't wait to get back to his job after the first ten days at home. 'Nothing to do in the village . . . everything so dirty . . . no proper lavatory, no running water . . . boring life.' At least he was being honest. Did he miss his wife? Kids? 'Sometimes,' he said, after much thought.

It's not all that different for hot-shot corporate executives flying around the world, cutting deals. They also get used to a certain pace and a certain space. They get restless at home. And, eventually, the wives also begin to show their impatience at having a husband hanging around when he ought to be mid-air on a plane. Things work fine for such couples when they see just about enough of one another. Anything more and tension builds up. They get used to doing things solo. Strange as it may sound, a lot of couples then start behaving solo, even though they are technically married! Problems arise only when togetherness is re-established or demanded.

A well-connected socialite lady of my acquaintance has got so used to her husband not

If long separations are unavoidable, make a set of rules about 'staying connected'. Don't look at those awful phone bills with horror— communication is your lifeline under the circumstances.

being around that whenever he does come to town, she feels disoriented and mildly annoyed. It's like an intruder walking in and disrupting the rhythm of the life she has successfully constructed with her kids, their friends and her own friends. 'I really don't need him anymore,' she says candidly. 'For a short transitional phase when the decision was taken by him to relocate, I missed him madly. I was panic-stricken at the thought of taking care of the family all by myself. I thought I wouldn't be able to cope, that I'd be terrified at night and that I'd miss him like crazy. Nothing of the sort happened!' On his part the husband says he too feels strangely liberated. 'It's nice to know you have a lovely wife and great kids somewhere in the world. But it's equally nice to be able to enjoy your independence. I have made a pretty interesting life for myself as a "married bachelor", and I wouldn't swap it for anything in the world.'

From that end of the spectrum to the life my young domestic has picked, essentially it's the same story. She works in our home and sees her husband twice a year. The kids divide their time between the village and Mumbai. Her in-laws look after them, while her husband tills their patch of land and toils in the fields. Radhabai says she does love him and her children, but now that she has become accustomed to the big-city life, modern sanitation and Sunday movies, she cannot think of giving it all up and moving back to the village. She likes her urban existence and the money she makes.

Doesn't she feel lonely? Miss her 'mard'? She laughs. 'What is there to miss? His drunken outbursts and beatings? His sexual demands? No, thank you. I can put up with that nonsense twice a year because I know at the end of twenty days I can escape and come back to Mumbai. If you ask me to tell you frankly, I'm now married to Mumbai. This is where I want to die!'

Of course, there are cases of long-distance marriages working out wonderfully well. I've interacted with senior lady bureaucrats who've told me about their postings in different districts all over India. Some of them had married colleagues who also were in transferable jobs. These remarkable men and women had evolved their own special system whereby they either manoeuvred postings in such a way that they were in the same town, or they took turns when it came to promotions, especially if kids were involved. A wife willingly sacrificed a fat promotion which involved a transfer, to prevent disrupting a child's crucial stage at school. Equally, husbands kept their smart career moves on hold to accommodate the family's needs.

These marriages were far more stable since they were built on a common agenda, with the couples knowing exactly what sort of adjustments and sacrifices were involved in their field of work. All of them took care to explain that it hadn't been easy, that the marriage had gone through very rocky patches which they'd jointly worked hard to get over in the best interests of all. Women touring constantly in the districts did experience intense loneliness and frustration, as did the men. But it was their deep understanding of each other's professional commitments that helped them to understand and accommodate one another.

Speaking for myself, I know that I would find it terribly hard to sustain the emotional intensity required to keep a full-blooded relationship alive and thriving with a missing partner. I get my nurturing, my sustenance from interaction, conversation, laughter, sulks, petulance, fights, tears, touch, cuddles—you know, the daily dramas that make up life. And while the old saying 'Out of sight, out of mind' may sound cruel, it is pretty accurate.

> *Don't make the missing partner feel guilty about extended absences—he/she will run in the opposite direction rather than be forced to deal with accusations of neglect.*

Which makes me wonder how the wives of those in the armed services spend years and years on their own, waiting for husbands who may or may not return. They have to be made of sterling stuff. I've seen young brides of our men in uniform, separated from their grooms months after the wedding. Some have kids who've never seen their fathers. The wives themselves barely know the men they married. And yet, nothing shakes their faith, nothing touches their loyalty. Who knows what actually transpires when the husbands get back, weary and forlorn? Do they reconnect immediately? Do they feel a sense of alienation, even despair? Do they wonder who the stranger is? Nobody will ever give you a candid response to these questions.

I've seen marriages that straddle continents, and those that start off as 'weekend marriages' and often end up as 'bi-monthlies'. Believe me, it's hard to keep emotions on course with more separations than togetherness. Women, in particular, miss the reassurance of a male presence at home. As one wife quipped, 'It's not that I'm helpless— far from it. I can handle anything . . . any crisis. I'm half a carpenter, a full mechanic, an excellent driver, gardener, cook and plumber. Even so, my first reaction when faced with a problem is, "I wish my husband were here—what am I going to do? Oh God . . . please help me." It's only when I'm calmer that I tell myself there's nothing he would have done differently. Perhaps there are a few things I can do better. What I actually miss is sharing the experience with him. Just knowing there's another person who'll be an equal partner in whatever the problem may be—even a pet dog's paw getting hurt—makes a huge difference.'

How right she is. As a senior flight stewardess put it, 'Of course life goes on . . . we all adjust, adapt. I fly more than ten days a month. I'm sure my family misses me, just as I miss them. But you know what? We get used to it. Human beings are like that—we get used to anything. In fact, because I'm gone so much, I try that much harder to please everybody when I'm home. And my family does the same.'

She had a point. We can get used to anything, and do. But I believe equally that marriage requires more than just a mental commitment. Couples, separated for any reason, claim they 'work harder' at their relationship. They have to. These couples point out how easy modern communication has made their lives, what a difference an SMS makes, how they can chat on-line for hours, no matter where they are in the world. 'In fact,' gushed a banker, 'I speak much more to my husband these days than I used to when both of us chose to stay in the same town. At some point, we discovered we weren't going anywhere professionally, and neither was our relationship. We were stuck and feeling bored. A certain staleness had set into the marriage. We decided to get back into the career-groove and—boom— we're fine. Yes, we miss each other, but it's great what instant connectivity can do. You should check our e-mails and messages—they're hot!'

Great. I'd like to speak to the same couple a few years from now and find out if the e-mails are still flying as passionately. If they are, I'll eat this book. I swear it. My guess is, either they will have split up and found other partners or one of them would have given up the frantic travel schedule to make a home. It's not possible to maintain such a crazy pace and still hang on to intimacy via computers or cellphones. This generation is looking for surrogate forms of nurturing relationships. I don't believe there's a good enough substitute for physical presence.

Yes, a marriage can endure with long absences and separate time zones—but that marriage eventually changes its character and becomes a comfortable arrangement between two people who are fine on their own but prefer being married, since they're used to the idea of being a couple and it's too much of a hassle to 'uncouple'.

I remember feeling alarmed when a young friend of mine started travelling on work for up to twenty days a month, leaving a dishy husband to fend for himself. Well, fend he most certainly did—with lots of help from nubile singles and the restless wives of common friends.

Under the guise of 'looking after' the deserted 'bachelor boy', the women took over his time, life, kids and home, making sure he didn't have a single evening to himself. He, of course, loved every minute of the extra attention and pampering. Initially, his wife was amused, grateful, even curious. She began to see her husband in a different light and liked what she saw. It added an extra zing to their marriage, which had fallen into a bit of a rut. The husband, too, liked his more mobile wife—it meant less nagging and better rapport. They could afford to be communicative over e-mail and SMS. Their messages were affectionate and sexy. Quite a different story from their earlier lives, when the wife snapped and the husband snarled. Both thought they were finally on to a good thing—they were certainly a whole lot happier. Till it dawned on the husband that sure, they were happier. But the reason for that was that they were happier on their own.

On her ten-day visits home, the old tensions still surfaced and buried hostilities bubbled over. The kids, too, were better off with Mom gone. Mainly because Dad was more chilled out and allowed them to do the sort of 'fun stuff' Mom was dead set against—in other words, they were left to themselves a lot, and how they loved their new-found freedom! Of course they missed Mom, but they also liked the shopping she arrived with. Besides, the atmosphere in the house was relaxed and easy. Even the domestics were in a better mood with memsaab gone. They could watch TV for hours, loll around and produce indifferent meals—who noticed? Who cared? Well, the mother-in-law did!

With years of experience behind her, the old girl finally raised an alarm and warned her daughter to slow down and assess the situation. She started a file of clippings that frequently 'caught' the husband on page three, partying with a crowd of attractive people—strangers to his wife.

Initially, the girl laughed off the 'threat' and told her mother she was reading too much into society gossip. But soon, she began to see a certain pattern. One or two of the female companions were constants. The husband had altered his way of dressing—it was younger, more clubby and definitely designed to impress. He seemed far more distracted as well and, worse, disinterested in sex. This, from a man who took enormous pride in his libido and insisted on energetic sex practically every day. As for her, she was far too jet-lagged to contemplate anything more strenuous than a hot shower and deep sleep when she was home. In other words, the marriage wasn't exactly rocking—it was on the rocks, more like.

At her mother's insistence, my friend altered her job profile and started spending more and more time at home. To her horror and disappointment, she discovered no one wanted her there any more—not even the kids, who had got accustomed to a laid-back, lenient lifestyle, with no deadlines, no restrictions. The husband's female friends actually voiced their resentment after a couple of stiff margaritas and told the wife she'd spoilt everybody's fun, including her own! 'We thought you guys had it all sorted— you did your thing at work and play. And he did his. Besides,

Self-sufficiency is the spin-off from such an arrangement. Separations have a way of making partners less dependent, less clingy, less demanding.

you weren't there when he needed you . . . or when your kids needed supervision.' The wife was shocked. She felt betrayed. She said, 'I thought I was doing all this for my family.' The husband put it in perspective when he said, 'No honey, you were doing it for yourself.'

The couple did the sensible thing. They sat down and talked. First to each other, and then to a professional counsellor. It wasn't too late, they concluded. And it wasn't. Today, they look back on those two years of 'madness' as they call it, and wonder how foolish they'd both been to believe it was possible to have it all. It never is.

In today's scenario, both partners have to constantly reaffirm their original commitment to one another. A lot may have changed (more mobility for women), but a lot hasn't (men still expect their wives to wait on them). Marriage thrives on old-fashioned nurturing. It always has, and always will. And that cannot happen via remote control. As for posting tantalizing messages in a chat room—beware, those can go astray. And a whole other cyber dimension could come into play.

Therefore:

- ♥ Couples should ideally refrain from being apart habitually. Why get married if you prefer to spend time on your own?
- ♥ If the wife's career involves travel to distant lands more

The Truth About Marriage

than ten days of the month, review the career or the marriage. Ditto for the husband.

- ♥ Men who travel stray. True? Broadly speaking, yes. Equally true about women who travel.

- ♥ Trust is important in the case of absentee partners. Do not play the ugly 'spy game' and keep suspecting the other. Don't become paranoid or cross-question, if you call and find the partner not in at some odd hour.

- ♥ Get a life. Adopt a healthy, positive approach to your partner's absence. Use your free time constructively to pick up a new skill—music, language, games, writing.

- ♥ If children are involved, make sure they don't forget the missing parent. Keep the person 'alive' by making kids reach out through cards, letters, messages, calls.

- ♥ The issue of sexuality is a trickier one to sort out—it depends entirely on mutual levels of sex drive, views towards fidelity and, finally, the confidence in each other. It's best to table your anxieties in this area boldly and freely.

- ♥ Find creative ways to keep the marriage going and to fan the flames of passion. Send each other erotic poetry. Exchange tantalizing messages. Cold comfort? Maybe. But it's still better than actual coldness and life in a deep freeze.

Twenty
The Dreaded C-word
Kabhi haan, kabhi naa

A young man was staring hard at holiday pictures of his parents. Said he to his mother, 'Hey, you don't look like you're having such a great time.' The mother shrugged, smiled and said mildy, 'Well, since you did notice—I wasn't! It really wasn't my idea of a holiday. Nothing about the plan interested me—neither the destination nor the culture. Frankly, I was bored and exhausted and dying to come home.'

The son looked up from the album and asked, 'Why did you agree to go? Why couldn't you have said no?' The mother waved her hand wearily. 'It's easier to go along—

you won't understand. Wait till you get married . . .'

The son shuddered. 'Thanks, but no thanks, if this is what it entails. I could never compromise. Your life has been one unending compromise—not worth it, yaar. Look at you . . . going along on a stupid vacation you didn't enjoy and which left you stressed. Why? Because you wanted to please Dad.'

The mother smiled. 'Nobody held a gun to my head, remember? I did it because I wanted to. Not everything in life is driven by self-interest. Yes, I did have a lousy time, but seeing your father happy and relaxed was in itself pretty satisfying. And don't forget, he goes along with a lot of my nonsense, too. That's what a partnership is all about.' The son looked unconvinced. He left the room shaking his head and muttering, 'Partnership, my ass. Sounds more like Dad bullying and having his own way as he generally does.'

This is but a tiny (and relatively unimportant) example of how a dirty word like 'compromise' can be misrepresented or misinterpreted. Rarely does one find a relationship so perfectly balanced, so well worked out that compromise doesn't become an issue at some time or the other. Who doesn't have to confront 'compromise' at various points in life? Whether it's with a business associate or a friend, compromise is an inevitability that can be handled with intelligence and grace. But it can also lead to conflict and an eventual rift. It all depends on how big the compromise is. Not being in sync over holiday destinations is a small issue. Couples often have to deal with far weightier ones.

Compromise need not be a dirty word if it works both ways— sometimes you give in, sometimes your partner does.

Take the case of Imran and Jemima Khan whose divorce made headlines internationally. I tried putting myself in Jemima's shoes: What if one fine day, my husband came to me and announced the arrival of a young girl (his love child) in our lives? No matter how liberal, large-hearted and progressive I may consider myself, I would have freaked out. And I would have asked my husband whether, had the situation been reversed, he would have found it within himself to accept my love child? The answer to that would probably have decided my course of action.

Compromising on basic values and principles is where I would draw the line. Compromise gets nasty when one person in the marriage turns around and says, 'Look, this isn't on. Enough is enough. I feel short-changed.' What then? I hear countless stories narrated by disgruntled men and women who talk bitterly about feeling betrayed by their partners. Modern urban marriage is such that one little let-down and the battle cry 'Let's call the lawyers' is promptly raised. If some of the issues seem foolish, self-generated and superficial, well, that's marriage for you, these days. But the bigger ones that need closer examination revolve around contemporary concerns like job transfers, relocation, kids and in-laws. These are not as easily resolved; working women, in particular, agonize over the countless 'compromises' they make (willingly or otherwise) at the office so as to cause least damage at home.

Women frequently let go of lucrative increments if they are linked with increased mobility or longer work-hours. But over time, a certain level of resentment builds up, regardless of what they may claim. The question of where to leave kids (if there are any) while mom goes to work often becomes a contentious issue (her parents or his?), and if these matters aren't thought through at the right time, they can lead to a breakdown of the relationship.

A career can be very demanding. To do full justice to a career and attempt to win awards as a brilliant homemaker is to ask for trouble. Couples have to be clear about their goals and priorities well before they put their feet into full-time jobs. Something generally gives—often it's the woman's resolve. 'I can't do it,' I recall a young banker crying. 'There's too much pressure. I feel I have to prove too much, both at home and at the office. At the end of all my efforts, nobody is happy and I'm exhausted and impatient most of the time. My husband and I hardly have time for each other. Sex? Forget it! Who has the energy?'

She was articulating what a lot of young careerists experience. When this woman gave up her well-paying job to stay home, it didn't solve anything. The word 'compromise' kept cropping up. She felt martyred and was filled with self-pity. The husband felt guilty and ended up resenting her so-called 'sacrifice'. Finally, he begged her to go back to work. She did so, but on a flexi-schedule. So far, they're still together and seem happy. But the wife often wonders: 'Why does it have to be me who's on flexi-time? I was earning as much; my career was zipping along at a faster pace than my husband's. I gave up my goals. What has he given up?'

Frankly, it's generally a win-win situation for men. Women who accept this as a hard-to-dismiss fact of life are generally better able to adapt and, yes, compromise. But I've seen it go in the other direction as well. Men who marry women with distinctly different interests and passions often start drifting after a few listless years of marriage. And, of course, vice-versa. A woman I know quite well is so dedicated to her sporty life, nothing else matters. If it's not golf, it's badminton; if it isn't that, it's swimming. When she's not at the club, she's jogging at the race course. She is maniacal about her workouts and personal training. Her husband's idea of a fitness regime is to lift his glass of beer to his lips over weekends. The two are entirely out of sync. She loves movies and music; he prefers crossword puzzles and history books. She enjoys dancing and people; he likes chess and cognac. They occupy different worlds and frequently find themselves in different time zones (both travel constantly). Yet, they say their marriage is as perfect as it can get. Maybe they're right. It depends on what you expect from marriage. If it's togetherness above all, with shared passions, this formula will not work for you. But if you agree that basic compatibility and a certain mutual regard is all it takes, this version of marriage is ideal.

Hit the delete button when it comes to ego. There's no shame in meeting your partner halfway.

'The less we see of each other, the more we value the time spent together,' a couple confessed over dinner. They looked genuinely happy and earnest while making this declaration. They ardently pursued their individual careers, interests and friends, and yet were equally comfortable sitting around at home, each in their own corner, the wife chatting on the computer, the husband watching a sports channel on TV. 'We've worked it out,' the wife often boasts. 'We like each other enough, but it's not as if we don't like other people as much. We made our adjustments early on in the marriage.'

The Truth About Marriage

For me, this kind of a format simply does not work. I like the idea of sharing and doing things together (up to a point, of course). I don't necessarily go along with all of my husband's interests. But, other than the odd weekend or two, I genuinely prefer doing stuff together. And nearly all decisions (major or minor) are taken jointly. I don't feel claustrophobic or hemmed in and I don't feel I'm missing out on any of the 'fun' my girlfriends tell me about. But that's also because none of these 'conditions' have been thrust on me.

I decide what I want to do with my time. This is more, much more, than what millions of women are technically 'allowed', either by their husbands or their families. When I'm asked about any compromises I might have made in my marriage, I'm frankly stumped. All the options I had by-passed had been discarded after weighing their importance in my life. Of course there have been opportunities I've turned down, a few I've even regretted turning down, but when I look back, I don't think of any of them as 'compromises' of the unpleasant sort.

Giving up something after a careful consideration of what it actually means to your life does not generate a feeling of loss. Initially, perhaps: petulance can be so attractive! But the valuable perspective that time provides generally gives one the answer. Was it worth it? If the response is 'yes', forget everything else and rejoice. The only compromises that any right-thinking person should reject are those that ask you to obliterate the very values that define you and form the backbone of your convictions.

A partner who asks you to be a party to a crime, sign false documents, lie, cheat, intimidate, deceive or indulge in any act that goes against your grain is asking for far too much. He or she is literally compromising your integrity, your essential self (and there are an astonishing number of people who think nothing of imposing these conditions). You have the right to refuse emphatically and stick to that decision, no matter what the consequences. Partners who adopt cheap tricks like 'That means you don't really trust me . . . and if you don't trust me, it means you don't love me either; or else, why would you question my motives?' should be promptly told when and where to get off. Alas, far too many women lack the courage or even the option to say 'no' when it comes to coercion of this kind.

- ♥ A reasonable amount of personal 'sacrifice' goes with the territory—accept it.
- ♥ It's wise to anticipate and review areas of major disagreement before they explode into conflict.
- ♥ Women who keep cribbing about being forced to 'compromise' are often attention-seekers who need martyrdom as a prop.
- ♥ There's no such thing as having it your way all the time.

The Truth About Marriage

Get real and accept the fact that you have to yield sometimes.

♥ Meet your partner halfway, even in matters that annoy or irritate you, like taking a (fake) interest in his or her interests. At least the effort is being made.

♥ Hold your ground when it comes to the big stuff. Don't buckle under pressure if your partner asks you to compromise your values, principles, or beliefs.

Twenty-one
All in the Family
Ghar ghar ki kahani

Not everybody is Laxmi Mittal. Not everybody can hire the gardens of the Versailles Palace and spend crores of rupees to marry off an adored daughter. But does that stop anyone from trying?

Marriages are no longer family functions which announce new beginnings for a couple. They're been converted into joint ventures, and like any JV, there are contractual problems that eventually ruin the honeymoon. Each time I pass the half-a-kilometre strip opposite Mumbai's famous 'Queen's Necklace' I see three, sometimes four enormous mandaps, the generator vans juicing up the power supply needed for all those blinding lights. The lakhs spent on flowers ('what, no orchids?'), some more lakhs on feeding hundreds of invitees (most of them strangers) and God knows how many zeroes added to the grand total (trousseau, gifts, jewels) and you have yourself a grand Indian wedding. Oh-oh, I forgot to include the pre- and post-shaadi extravaganzas, which, these days, rival the best that Bollywood throws up.

Naturally, since that's where it all began, with a film called *Hum Aapke Hain Kaun*. I've named and nailed the culprit. Now every wedding (even that one in the burbs) boasts a mandatory 'sangeet', complete with synchronized dancing by the entire family (yes sir, chachas, chachis, masis and mamajis), matching outfits, hired choreographer (they don't call them dance masters any more), professional video cameramen to record these shenanigans for posterity, and if you can afford it, an 'item girl' to perform the latest cabaret on stage!

So fierce is the competition and so intense the pressure, that no family today can escape the five-day tamasha, which includes an elaborate mehendi ceremony, a youngsters' cocktail party, an Oldies' Nite and God knows how many lunches and dinners in between. This is not elite South Mumbai speak. Trust me. Even small towns in India take their cues from Big City madness and the name for the current madness is 'shaadi'. I really don't know who enjoys this rubbish, and I've made it amply clear to my own kids where I stand on the issue. Not that they're listening. I fear when the moment of truth arrives, I too shall be bullied into obliging either my children or the families of their 'chosen ones'.

I try and point to my own wedding, which couldn't have been celebrated in a simpler fashion. Never mind that my shaukeen husband followed up the charming, minimalistic temple courtyard ceremony with a sit-down dinner in a ballroom. As a new bride, I didn't want to frighten him with my adamant attitude to the sheer waste. He isn't all that easy to convince or bulldoze once his mind is made up, anyway. But the ceremony itself was conducted as per my wishes, under an open sky, with no more than fifty invitees.

My children look bored and unimpressed when I show them the pictures. 'What's the point?' they ask. 'Weddings should be fun.' Well, that depends on how one describes 'fun', I guess. I recoil in horror at the thought of undertaking a five-day circus. But I guess I'll survive, as countless mothers do.

'Joint family? Eeeks! No way, man,' is how a young girl responded when I raised the topic. She added, 'I don't want to be told what to wear, what to do, what to eat, how to behave . . . I want my marriage to be a chilled out zone. I want total freedom to live, dress and eat as I please. If I want to smoke, it's not while hiding in the bathroom. If I want a drink, I don't want to conceal it in a cola. If I want to call my friends over, I want them to feel comfortable. If I want to wear skimpy outfits, or backless cholis . . . I don't want to be glared at by my in-laws. It's my life . . .'

Don't try and score brownie points over your mother-in-law. Give her the entire cookie jar, instead!

The girl was clear and candid. Our traditional joint-family with all its so-called 'virtues' and 'values' was not for her. And millions of young Indians like her feel the same way about opting out of an institution that has been around since the days of the *Mahabharata*.

One thing I'm certain about—the happy days of well-adjusted joint families living in harmony with two, even three generations, are over. I definitely don't think such a situation would work for me and have told my kids so. Today, 'space' is what we all crave for—physical and emotional. Physically, modern apartments can barely contain four adults, without everybody tripping over everybody else. With the disappearance of sprawling family homes and the switchover to urban rat-holes, it's tough enough for a family to hang in there. Throw in a bahu and you get an Ekta Kapoor serial.

The reason all these dismal saas-bahu family soaps work

big time is because in their own absurd way they reflect the truth. Let's face it, that old way of life, with clearly demarcated hierarchies and roles, is over. Expecting today's young woman to adapt, obey and still smile, is asking for the moon, sun and entire galaxy. She is her own person and it's foolish to expect her to conform to a lifestyle she may not wish to be a part of. Why, even my own mother, sixty-odd years ago, was bold enough to tell my father she wasn't ecstatically happy sharing her life with strangers who weren't all that nice to her. My father, bless him, understood her discomfort and sensibly took a job in New Delhi. I know she would have been an entirely different woman had she stayed within the confines of my father's extended family. The well-timed move to New Delhi saved her, nurtured the marriage, and indirectly saved all her kids, me included.

I feel a little sorry for modern girls who are not given a choice in this key decision. If they have to become a part of the Great Indian Family, my advice is this: don't buck the system. Subvert it subtly, instead. Live in peace, live with a smile on your face. There's nothing more off-putting to a young husband than the sight of a sour-puss, waiting for him to get home so she can bitch, bitch, bitch about his family. Even if he loves his bride to death and is her ghulam, at some point he is going to resent her nagging criticism and start feeling alienated.

The Truth About Marriage

Intrigue, jealousy, competitiveness, back-biting, tale-carrying, sabotage and stealth-attacks are all a part of life in a joint family. If you find yourself in one, remember you aren't alone—countless women are in the same situation, and feeling the same way: hostile, let down, rejected, dejected, humiliated, frustrated and angry. Very angry. The senior members of the joint family are not going to change for you. It is you who will have to change. Accept that and you won't feel suicidal. Better still, concentrate on creating good will without expecting applause for every little gesture. The onus of integrating with your new family rests with you.

This basic issue (to live with his family) must be sorted out at the very beginning of the courtship. So should the question of how exactly the marriage is to be conducted—scale, expense, religious vows. Table everything. Every little thing. Invest time and thought well in advance, so that there's no ambiguity. If you abhor big, fussy weddings, say so and arrive at a compromise. If you want to keep it simple and it's a matter of principle to you, say that too. Meet your in-laws half-way, just to prove your positive attitude to the match. But once a decision is taken, don't crib, especially not to your partner.

'Grace' is the key. Weddings always show people up and are necessarily complicated. Focus on the good stuff and cope with the bad, as best as you can. Stereotypes need to be broken. You don't have to behave as though you are in one of those wretched, saas-bahu sagas.

Joint families do have their advantages if you know how to negotiate your way through landmines. I know a few young girls who married into large, extended families, and seem to be perfectly well-adjusted and happy. Modern-day ma-in-laws come with a built-in cool quotient, and don't oppress the new entrant as they once were known to.

Some brides claim they prefer this arrangement since they don't have to bother with domestic duties. Kitchen politics—the frequent family-spirit killers—are left to the older generation, so the younger bahus feel freed

Leave your husband out of daily squabbles. Bickering over unimportant stuff like who gets to holiday and where, is silly and counterproductive.

from spending hours agonizing over bhindi and chicken decisions. They also say that the joint family works best in times of crises—deaths, emergencies, births, travel. 'Everybody comes together at such times. I find so much support, just in terms of additional infrastructure, hands and minds. People can be so very helpful when you most need help,' said a grateful bahu, recounting how willingly the entire family had helped out when her brother met with an accident on the highway.

That's the upside. Of course, there will be problems. Competition between bahus, for one, and the fact that tact is required at all times when one is dealing with so many different personalities living under the same roof. The division of duties and the distribution of money become primary concerns.

Today's girls find it embarrassing, even humiliating, to have to ask their in-laws for funds. Or to have to share the car-pool. Career bahus, in particular, don't like to surrender their pay cheques and then wait for hand-outs. And more important than any of this is an issue that's rarely addressed, because of the shame involved—sexual exploitation. Somehow, joint families make it harder for bahus to handle unwanted sexual advances from their husband's family—it could be a brother-in-law, a cousin-in-law, an uncle-in-law or even the father-in-law. What does the bahu do? Most times she remains silent, too shocked or embarrassed to deal with such an uncomfortable situation. This awful phenomenon is more widespread than society will allow us to believe.

I firmly believe that the conspiracy of silence surrounding the subject must be violated as forcefully as the perpetration of the ghastly act itself. Women have to find the courage to speak up and expose the person subjecting them to the abuse. The husband has to be told.

And don't worry about his reaction. He may go into instant denial and say, 'What nonsense! You are imagining it! Such things don't happen. My family members are not like that. How dare you make such an accusation?' Be prepared for this and insist on a solution to the problem. Confront the villain along with your husband. I know it isn't easy. But it must be done.

Even though joint families are slowly disappearing, one has to accept the fact that for a large percentage of Indians, it's a system that has endured and worked. Even with all its failings, the joint family is not about to disappear entirely. We may as well accept that girls who marry into one, have to abide by the rules of the family without straining at the leash too much. Focus on the advantages instead, and don't deny your own identity. While joint families don't encourage displays of great individuality, it's still possible to assert yourself within prescribed parameters. Don't despair if your life is monitored a bit too closely for comfort. Think, instead, that you are spared the tedium of looking for the perfect baingans to smoke for bhartha at the Sunday family lunch.

In the interests of peace:

- ♥ Play ball with your in-laws. Joint-family life isn't easy. But it isn't all that terrible, either.
- ♥ Focus on the advantages of being a Bade Parivaar ki

Bahu. Don't exaggerate the disadvantages.

♥ Fighting over non-issues ('Bhabiji took the car when I needed it to go to the mandir'), is a dumb thing to do. Organize your resources in a spirit of co-operation, not one-upmanship.

♥ There's no need to get over-chummy with in-laws, even if they are really amazing. A certain healthy distance is good for such tricky relationships.

♥ If you are very sure you'll never be able to adjust, compromise or conform to joint-family life, state your case at the very beginning and stick to the decision.

♥ Wedding ceremonies are super extravaganzas these days. If you prefer something more discreet, speak up.

♥ Don't start wedded life on a sour note, quibbling over wedding expenses. Be upfront and adhere to budgets, once you've frozen arrangements.

♥ Dowry? Are you nuts! The minute that ghastly word is referred to, and demands made—cancel the wedding!

Twenty-two
Managing Ma-in-law
Mere paas ma hai

How to manage your mother-in-law? Don't laugh! Just do it.

You think I'm joking when I say a mother-in-law can be trained if you know the right tricks? Why not? She's only human. And susceptible to stuff other humans succumb to—flattery, gifts, praise, affection, obedience, respect. Convert her into a monster in your mind and she'll turn into one. Treat her like an adversary and she'll behave like one. Be yourself with her and chances are, she'll accept you for who you are, sooner or later. Don't play games, don't pretend, don't be a bloody hypocrite.

Mothers-in-law are the most maligned people on earth—they have to put up with nasty jokes, cartoons, misrepresentation in movies and, of course, deep-rooted prejudice. They're expected to be scheming, nasty, devious and possessive creatures, whose sole objective in life is to destroy their daughters-in-law. This is utter rubbish, especially today, when the ma-in-law is herself a hot and happening person with a life of her own.

The worst thing you can do when you become part of a new family is to get your ma-in-law's back up by not acknowledging her position within the family. Hierarchy still matters, and you have to remember she's senior in both age and experience. Defer to her, learn from her, befriend her and soon you'll be cracking jokes about the man you share—your husband.

I'm waiting to become a mother-in-law myself and hence can afford to preach. It is also true that I'm instinctively suspicious of any girl dating either one of my two sons. 'You scare all our girlfriends off. They refuse to come home,' my sons tell me. That's when I stop dead in my tracks, stare hard at the mirror, look into my own eyes and say, 'You too . . .?' The answer depresses me. Yes, me too!

The fact is that for every vamp, there are at least four decent, caring and smart women who do not feel threatened or displaced by their bahus. When co-existence is inevitable, these women understand the importance of co-opting the bride in a pleasant way. 'I have my life, she has hers. We don't interfere or get into each other's hair,' says an enlightened neighbour whose son got married recently. 'In fact, I'm so sensitive to my daughter-in-law's needs, I constantly instruct the cook to make all her favourite dishes. I work. She works. Both of us are too busy to argue or fight.'

Now, there's a sensible lady. I've met her bahu, who is like any other career girl these days. 'She leaves home at 9 a.m. and returns around 7 p.m. And often, before I know it, my son and she have gone out again. Drinks . . . dinner . . . movie . . . play. I don't ask and they don't tell.'

Does she feel left out? 'Sometimes. But I also realize they have their own priorities. The fun will start when they decide to have kids. I refuse to be their full-time nanny!'

'Good for you,' I said to her. Any major disagreements? 'Not so far. Money is an issue. My daughter-in-law expects me to subsidize her extravagant lifestyle . . . two foreign holidays a year, a new car . . . I don't say no. But I don't say yes, either.'

The son plays a passive role and is clever enough not to play refree. Does this lady feel mothers-in-law are unfairly represented? 'Definitely. My own mother-in-law was a loving person who never came in my way. In fact, I depended on her much more than I did on my own mother. It was she who saw me through my pregnancy.'

No matter how many certificates enlightened mothers-in-law give themselves, as far as popular culture is concerned, they are still a bad influence. Most TV soaps concentrate obsessively on a demonic representation of the species, and most films reinforce it. Women-who-lunch spend a good part of the afternoon criticizing their own. And harassed husbands complain they can deal with virtually

Mothers-in-law should kill with kindness and generosity. Don't give your heart to your bahu, but hand over everything else. You'll feel so much lighter!

everything else, but not the unending stream of invectives against their mothers. Women should know that it's a lousy habit and they should refrain from running the old girl down. The old girl, too, should wake up and smell the coffee, if she thinks today's daughter-in-law is going to meekly follow her diktat. Girls who are in a position to walk rather than suffer do just that. Or ask to move into their own homes.

Meanwhile, there is a happier meeting ground. Since both women are likely to be usefully occupied these days, they can mark out their territories and evolve a system that works for both. Even domestic 'duties' can be shared if the attitude is right.

Not having had too much experience in this department, I can only provide an optimistic forecast. When I get to mother-in-law mode, I would want to treat my bahu with the same sort of respect I seek. I would give her time to get used to the family and our way of life. And I would remind her that she's married to our son—not us. I would urge her to pursue her career, if she has one, or any interests that occupy her time productively. I have seen something new in this area—saas-bahu business combos. And they seem to be working just fine!

Inclusion rather than exclusion should be the mantra to follow. As the older, more experienced woman, it is the mother-in-law's responsibility to make all the first moves. She has to remind herself that her daughter-in-law is entering a new zone. The younger woman's insecurity levels are that much higher. Reassurance on a day-to-day level is all she requires. Praise her efforts to please, give her the opportunity to learn the rules of your family. Give her time. And mainly, give her encouragement. I don't think that's too much to ask. She will be eternally grateful and you will have earned your girl-scout points.

This is the age of breaking antiquated moulds and rules. Power games have no place in a home. Mothball your ego and reach out. A smiling bahu is better than a weeping one. When that slightly burnt khichdi is served to you at the dinner table, don't be a hypocrite and shower praise on the miserable dish. That's far more insulting than telling your bahu what is wrong with the recipe and how she can fix it. Make a light joke about the mess and discreetly pick up the phone to order a pizza, dosa or Chinese takeaway. If you have a daughter yourself, imagine her in a similar situation. And you won't go wrong.

In case your bahu happens to be an ace bitch, playing hard politics and deliberately wrecking the peace in your family, then sit her down and engage her in a no-nonsense one-on-one. Tell her plainly where she needs to get off and explain how it actually works in your parivaar. If she's clever (and a survivor), she'll get the message loud and clear. If not, you might have to take a few hard decisions regarding alternative living arrangements, either for yourself or your son.

To be a good mother-in-law, you have to tell yourself there is really no other option. Today's bahus are hardly likely to put up with the old nonsense. They will either walk out (in which case, your son will hate you forever), or they will take you on. Be sensible. After all, you are older and more experienced. Even if you, yourself, have been at the receiving end of ghastly treatment from your saas, you must not repeat the pattern.

Winning over the woman your son loves is easier said than done. Let's be honest, there is that nasty business of possessiveness, jealousy and competition. The darling little boy who always came to you for everything now dances to another woman's tune. You start feeling excluded and left out. Worse, you start believing he no longer needs you or loves you. This isn't at all true. He does. And he will continue to. Provided you don't behave churlishly or childishly. His attention will naturally be focused on his bride. If you indulge his besotted state and treat his love-sickness with grace, he will appreciate your accommodation and be grateful for it in years to come. So will the bride.

What the young couple desperately need is some space, physical and emotional. They are getting used to each other and making necessary adjustments. It is your delicate handling of this period that will determine the foundation of their relationship. Bite your tongue before criticizing him or her. Teach her the ways of your khandaan without making her feel alienated or ignorant.

A newly married woman told me recently how humiliated she felt when she wasn't consulted even once during a family function. All the other women got together to plan various ceremonies and organize their clothes and jewellery. She was treated like a snoop or an unwanted stranger. 'I was made to feel like an interloper . . . nobody asked for my opinion. Nobody was interested in what I was going to wear for the function . . . nor did anyone check whether I needed anything . . . maybe some family jewellery. I just sat in my room while the others laughed and enjoyed themselves.' I completely understood the young girl's sense of rejection. How on earth would she ever feel like an accepted member of her new family if this was their attitude?

The bride reasoned, 'Maybe it's a community thing. You see . . . I don't belong to theirs!' Well, all the more reason to include her, I would think. But, as she put it, 'They are so clannish and closed. Also, so very formal. I was raised very differently. My mother's was an open house. My sister-in-law still gets preference over me. My mom gives her the first pick of everything—clothes, jewellery, food. But, in my husband's family, they are very conscious of hierarchy. I'm the first girl from a different caste and community to marry into their family. It will take them time to accept me. I'll have to make more of an effort myself . . . try harder . . . adjust.' I remembered this lovely girl as a happy teenager in faded jeans. Today, she cannot leave her bedroom without changing into a saree, covering her head and wearing appropriate jewellery. Oh yes, she also has to touch her mother-in-law's feet each morning!

Talking to a delightful group of students in Jaipur, I recounted this story and they laughed. 'It's the same for all of us. Our parents want us to marry by the age of nineteen, and hand over our lives to our mother-in-law. We are mentally geared for it.' Well, what can one say? If these girls have accepted such a passive role in their married lives, who can challenge it? Perhaps it's better this way. Less trouble for all. Mothers-in-law get a terrible name, regardless. And it's not just in India.

Daughters-in-law need to think about their own attitudes, too. And meet the old girl halfway, when possible. The worst thing to say to a young girl is: 'You must adjust.' Hey, she isn't an elastic band. Why should she be the only one 'adjusting'? Most fights occur over power and control. Mothers-in-law who refuse to give the keys to their daughters-in-law make the girls feel like petty thieves out to loot the family. Older women need to show more grace, more intelligence. This goes for kitchen politics, too. It's really not on to criticize the bahu's cooking or overrule her instructions to the staff. It's

Remember, it's difficult for a mother to 'surrender' her son to a 'stranger'. Deal with her initial hurt with understanding and patience—for your own sake.

demeaning and hurtful, since it automatically reduces both ma-in-law and bahu in the eyes of the household. If there are two or more daughters-in-law staying under the same roof, then, of course, it's a real conflict zone, with ma-in-law projected as the she-devil, playing games and manipulating the women to suit her own ends. This leads to ugly fights between brothers and eventually, even innocent kids of warring couples get entangled in the web. My advice to the saas-bahu scenario, twenty-first century-style, is as follows:

- ♥ Stay out of each other's hair as much as possible.
- ♥ Don't fight over bhindis and kaddus. Reserve your energy for something weightier. Carats over carrots, honey!
- ♥ Don't drag that milksop into your fights. There's no fate worse for a son/husband than to be caught in a cat-fight between his mom and wife.
- ♥ Follow a basic mantra: hold on to your temper. Count to five hundred if need be. Bite that sharp tongue and swallow those harsh words—they help nobody.
- ♥ Share your clothes with ma-in-law. It will make her feel young, hip and cool. Offer her your best designer shades, Chanel bag, Prada sandals. Take her shopping with your girlfriends.
- ♥ Join ma-in-law's kitty party group. Dazzle those ladies with Bollywood gossip (make it all up!). They'll love you for tolerating and entertaining them.
- ♥ Holiday together once every two or three years. It's amazing what an exotic resort, a few Kaiporishkas and a great tan can do to break the most formidable barriers.
- ♥ Flirt with your father-in-law. Flatter him shamelessly. But use utter discretion while you are at it. Don't send

out the wrong message, or else you might start something you won't be able to stop!

- ♥ Observe family rules and timings to the extent possible. Don't flout the authority of elders. Conform in the interests of peace within the family. But make sure to let your hair down in the privacy of your own space. We all need our safety-valves!

- ♥ Participate in family functions with humility. Fake it, if you have to. Learn from the old girl—she'll teach you a trick or two worth mastering.

- ♥ Bond with the best! There will always be an ally or two in a joint family. Build on those relationships and the rest will fall in line.

- ♥ Observe the dress code of the family to the extent possible. Don't hang around in skimpy shorts or tiny bustiers as you may have done in your own home. Dress appropriately at family functions—remember you aren't an 'item girl'.

- ♥ Pamper your ma-in-law with perfume and lingerie. Buy her the latest jeans, two sizes smaller than hers. She'll feel flattered enough to gift you an heirloom instantly.

- ♥ Don't compete, ladies. If the bahu prefers lasagna over sarson-da-saag, so be it.

- ♥ Make gajar-halwa especially for your bahu. Do something to make her feel wanted and loved. Offer to massage her hair with warm almond oil. Or book joint appointments for spa treatments. Learn to chill together!

♥ If you can survive a joint family, you can survive anything—even a nuclear war. Joint-family life prepares you for virtually anything. Make the most of all the varied experiences. Learn to cope, cajole and co-exist.

♥ Don't go crying to mama each time you have an argument with your spouse or in-laws. Learn to deal with such upheavals on your own. You are a big girl now—stop carrying tales like a school-kid.

♥ As for you, young man, I wish you good health, nerves of steel, enormous patience and . . . permanent deafness!

Twenty-three
Baby Talk
Hum do, hamarey do

Yeah, yeah, yeah. We all know what a pregnant woman is supposed to feel about her body when it bloats. How low her self-esteem sinks, how 'unsexy' she thinks she looks, how nothing turns her on, how her entire focus shifts to the life within, how excluded her husband feels, how so many marriages collapse during this 'ungainly' period in a woman's life, how most men can't bear the thought of sleeping with a woman as large as a house, how hypersensitive a mother-to-be becomes, how 'afraid' first-time parents are of hurting the unborn baby by having sex, how life changes dramatically, radically and forever, once a baby arrives. Well, here's the bad news—almost all of it is true. And the good? Babies can often become the best bond between couples, if you know how to work babies, motherhood, fatherhood and parenting into your married life.

The first thing about babies is, you must want them. If there is resistance to the idea itself, postpone the decision to have a child. Think about it carefully, think it through. It's a major decision which, once taken, is irreversible. You can't afford a 'rethink' once the deed is done. And yes, the arrival of a bawling baby into your life is definitely going to turn life itself on its head, at least for the first few years. Once you know the deal and like the terms, then go for it.

Couples who regard a child as anything less than a joy in their lives should ask themselves a thousand times whether it's worth bringing a 'semi-wanted' individual into the world. The trend these days is to postpone the decision—often till it's too late to have a biological offspring. Or not have a kid at all. Of the two, the second one is more sensible—at least you know your mind, have thought about the issue and decided child-rearing is not for you. Far better in the long run.

There are couples who are so 'complete' in themselves, they don't feel the need to alter the delicate balance by raising kids. I've seen several such marriages working out wonderfully well. No kids? No problem. This option was not available to an earlier generation. Couples were questioned by concerned elders: 'Is something wrong? Why are you still childless? Have you had a check-up? Tch-tch. God's curse.' Today, several professionals I know first make it clear that it's going to be a DINK (Double Income No Kids) story for them. If eyebrows are raised, they're also ignored. 'We enjoy each other's company enough, thank you. There's no space in our lives for a kid,' they state flatly.

It's the ones who go in for a family who sometimes end up wondering whether it was such a great idea after all. Especially the women, who can't stop lamenting over their 'ruined figure'. To them I say, which age, which world are you living in? Look at some of our glamorous actresses, models and VJs—mothers all. Getting your body into shape is entirely in your own hands. If it matters to you all that much, work out, eat smart and regain your old muscle tone. It's possible. And it's advisable, regardless of what your husband feels about it.

Through all my pregnancies, I ate like an ox. I used to think, what's the point in getting pregnant if you can't over-indulge and do so without guilt? It is only during those few months that a woman can stop obsessing about her altered silhouette and let go. I did this with the confidence that I would start a fitness regimen right after the delivery and stick to it. The thought of depriving myself, starving or agonizing over a few extra kilos here and there did not arise. As for the desirability factor, trust me, there are enough men in the world who find the sight of a pregnant woman entirely amazing and terribly attractive! It's what you feel about yourself that matters.

Couples should discuss all these concerns candidly. After all, the husband has had a starring role to play in this joint production. If he, for any reason, is put off by a large belly and breasts that display veins, either he should reorient his thinking and make a conscious effort to not show his revulsion, or he should discuss his reservations frankly with his wife. The last few months of being 'heavy with child' are tough enough for a mom-to-be without an insensitive husband adding to her woes. This time should be converted into a beautiful, mellow, communicative phase filled with tenderness, concern and gentle sex. Though doctors say it's okay to indulge in penetrative sex throughout pregnancy, I'd say, be cautious at all times. A tongue can be used for more than just talking, you know. There are several ways to achieve a climax without risking any possible harm to either yourself or the baby.

> *Competing for your attention with a new-born is a no-win situation for the poor husband. Don't allow that to happen. Get him to participate, instead.*

It's the period immediately following childbirth that most men find the hardest to deal with. For one, they are completely excluded from the rituals surrounding the mother. In so many Indian families, mother and child are packed off to the maternal home straight from the nursing home. A young husband begins to see this as the first rejection (unconsciously, of course). He gets to visit his wife and child, but it's obvious he isn't really needed. He generally hangs around wondering what to do with himself while the in-laws (and his own parents) fuss over the new arrival and his wife. With time on his hands and nothing to contribute, he starts hanging around with his buddies—bachelor friends from college, or single colleagues. He gets invited by other couples who tease him about becoming a father. Nobody actually tries to understand his confusion or his mixed feelings. Not even his wife, who's too busy with the baby.

It's important to be sensitive to the man's point of view at this crucial stage in his life. A woman who reaches out consciously and engages her husband in the care of the child (even if she has to act like mad!) is not being a hypocrite, she is being considerate. An 'inclusive' attitude is a far more positive way of tackling the situation. On his part, the bewildered young father should reassure his wife. She can't be feeling all that alluring or desirable, post-delivery. Chances are, she'll be living in ungainly, unflattering housecoats, caftans and nighties, with barely any time to groom herself or even run a comb through her hair. It is now that she needs her husband to hold her and tell her how lovely she looks (his turn to act!). If they convey just one thing to each other ('We're in this together'), the baby won't be seen as a barrier in their relationship.

For infants do take up a huge amount of the mother's time. She may not be able to join the husband in many of the activities they had enjoyed before the baby's arrival. The husband should understand, accept and make allowances. If he prefers to go on that trek by himself, he should. No point staying back and sulking. Similarly, if she wants time off to read a book, listen to music, or chill with her own friends, she should. Anything that contributes to peace and harmony between the couple. He should refrain from cutting jokes about her size ('I'll have to buy two airline tickets for her. She can't possibly fit into a single seat . . . just look at her'), and not show how squeamish he feels when she's cleaning up the baby or breast-feeding.

A young mother needs some fuss to be made over her after all that she's gone through. As for the man, who cannot (or will not) handle the nitty-gritties of caring for an infant, the least he can do is pamper the mom a little, spend time with her, take (or fake) an interest in the baby, help by fetching things like bottles, powder, towels, nappies.

The thing is to look interested and involved even if you initially feel entirely disconnected from the whole baby business. It's your kid, too, remember? If the very sight of the wriggly, squirming, screaming creature repulses you, remember it's quite normal to feel put off, even resentful and jealous of the attention the new arrival gets from your wife and the rest of the family. Don't suppress these feelings or pile on the guilt. Deal with the new situation, rely on humour, and let your wife know what you're experiencing. The minute you involve her in your confusion, she'll stop feeling so isolated and ignored. In fact, she may help you overcome your initial resistance, so that a few months down the line, you'll actually start engaging in the process of child-rearing in a more pro-active, positive way.

Making your wife feel loved and sexually attractive during these crucial months is very important. Small gestures can go a long way in this—buy her flowers or her favourite magazine, order in her favourite snack, hire DVDs she enjoys, or play music that reminds you both of earlier, more romantic times. She must not feel 'alone' during this period, or be left to the solicitous care of in-laws and family. She needs you more than ever, especially if she's suffering from post-delivery blues (millions of women feel vaguely, inexplicably depressed after giving birth). If she is in that frame of mind, don't tell her to 'snap out of it', because she can't. Don't ask dumb questions like 'If you didn't want the baby, why did you have it?' It isn't about the baby, or you. It's about her, and the feelings are too complex to sort out.

If your wife sounds weepy and irrational, be patient and calm. It will pass. All she needs is a little time to herself (the one thing a demanding infant denies her), and a little tenderness, a little understanding from you. If you feel irritated and unable to help, then do her and yourself a huge favour by leaving her alone. Don't lecture, preach, correct or criticize.

Motherhood, for many women, is a life-transforming experience, and perhaps the single most important aspect of their existence. A man who understands and appreciates this will go a long way towards strengthening the relationship. Any attempt to demean her emotions in this respect will damage your future. Think of a female tigress guarding her cubs, and beware. Never trifle or interfere with a woman's bond with her child—you do so at your own peril. It is a sacred bond that no man can ever dilute or devalue. The best approach is to put your own priorities on hold for a few months. That gives sufficient time to both to get used to a new pattern, a new rhythm.

Lives definitely get reorganized after the birth of a child. Accept that. And know for yourself that these changes are permanent and irreversible. Rejoice in the birth of your child and reap the results for life. Resent the presence, and live to rue the day you made the decision to go ahead and have one.

Oh yes, it's important during the pregnancy for a husband to read up on the subject. I'm always astonished and embarrassed by the high levels of ignorance displayed by dads-to-be. I wonder, are they so disinterested in their own progeny? Should they not be curious? Don't they want to know what's going on inside their wife's head, heart and body?

I recommend two books which I consider mandatory reading: the old dependable Dr Spock with its classic wisdom and *Everywoman* (there's also *Everyman*). Armed with these, you'll better understand the process of motherhood, and all the

Make the effort to dress and look the way you usually do. Pregnancy and childbirth are not afflictions to be endured. You should be looking your best during this period.

dramatic changes that occur within a woman's body. Add to these the psychological shifts, and you know that a baby is not just a new member being added to the family. A baby is an entirely new dimension to your life, often so radical in its impact, the dynamics of your relationship could change irrevocably. Don't let anybody underplay the significance of a baby—especially the first one. You get it right at that stage, and you'll get it right forever more. This isn't meant to scare you, but only to point out how far-reaching the impact actually is.

Mutual sensitivity is all that you need. A young mother must not get so self-obsessed and inward-looking that she forgets to pay attention to her husband, who may be feeling slightly lost and left out himself. If he appears perplexed, she must not accuse him instantly of neglect. If he seems distracted and disinterested in sex—it's not easy to get turned on by bulging contours and engorged breasts—don't fret. And don't rush into crazy diets and punishing fitness routines, out of fear that your husband might stray.

In India, of course, the problem is usually the opposite: Women let themselves go completely, because they believe it's 'natural' to put on those kilos after delivery. Sorry, it's not natural at all. It's lazy. A reasonable amount of weight-gain, especially for nursing mothers, is understandable. But it's equally important to get back into shape and tone up your muscles, once you stop breast-feeding. It is important from the point of view of your own health to get back into shape and refocus on yourself.

In my mother's time, women with babies stopped bothering about their weight and appearance, since they believed they'd done their 'duty' as married ladies, by producing heirs and spares to keep the bloodline going. They stopped viewing themselves as sexually active individuals and generally associated prosperity with *avoirdupois*. Fat deposits went hand in hand with bank deposits. We don't know what their husbands felt about the plumper silhouettes but, my guess is, since the wife's extra kilos were equated with the husband's success, the man was fine with it.

This attitude does not work any more. When I see young wives who have given up the fat-fight and have surrendered to those heavy-duty calories settling permanently on their middles, I feel like issuing a health warning. Conversely, when I see anorexic moms who start resembling dried twigs months after a baby, I want to make them share at least one full and satisfying meal with me if only to wipe that miserable, famished, deprived look from their faces. I strongly believe an over-exercised woman on a permanent diet, who believes in self-punishing regimes to stay fashionably thin, can never be a relaxed, fulfilled companion to anyone, least of all her long-suffering husband.

A hungry woman is an unhappy woman. All she has on her mind is food—not sex, not conversation, not love. To make things worse, she probably has bad breath and dark rings under her eyes. Why is this woman so unattractive? Because she is only really interested in herself. There's no time in her life for anyone—least of all a demanding baby. Either way (too much weight or too little), young mums need to straighten out their priorities and stick to a sensible middle-path. The weight will melt away over time, provided you maintain a smart eating plan and a simple exercise routine. Involve your husband. Work out together. Light exercises immediately after delivery are a great way of bonding and getting back together as a couple.

It's equally important to work around the baby's schedule once it's established. Steal those precious half-hours whenever you can, to concentrate exclusively on each other—chill, chat, snack, listen to music, touch and cuddle . . . at all times, express your love. It is only in such a nurturing environment that the newborn too will pick up positive signals and thrive.

To enjoy your pregnancy fully:

- Never exclude your partner from this, the most important development in your life.
- Accept the fact that the arrival of a baby changes everything. And forever. Don't fight this elementary truth.
- Avoid hierarchies. It isn't about assigning positions ('The baby comes first . . .' 'Nothing is as important as the baby . . .' 'Sorry, you'll have to wait for your turn').
- While weight gain is inevitable, it's not permanent. Don't make that extra weight an issue in your marriage. After all, what's gained can also be lost, over time.

- A baby has a way of devouring all your time. But it's important to reserve a portion for yourself and for your partner.

- Forget all those western 'rules' about equal sharing— it just doesn't happen here. Don't force your husband to stay up nights or change nappies if he doesn't want to. Coercion will only put his back up—and that's counter-productive.

- Slouching around in shabby nighties and housecoats, with uncombed hair and a stressed-out expression, is not likely to make your husband want to come rushing home. Wear lipstick, apply a little kajal, dress in practical but cheerful clothes if you're nursing the baby.

- Pregnancy does not automatically mean abstinence. On the contrary, this is the time when a woman needs reassurance the most. She must be made to feel desirable and wanted, even if sexual relations are restricted for medical reasons.

- Post-delivery is a particularly delicate period, when millions of women suffer from bouts of depression and low self-worth. It's important to see your partner over this hump.

- Small gestures—even an extra SMS or two during the day—assume a lot of importance, when a young mother's life revolves around feeds and nappy changes. Make the effort to indulge her small fancies—even an unexpected bar of chocolate can sometimes do the trick.

♥ A husband who succeeds in making his wife feel 'sexy' even when she's as big as a house, demonstrates his love for her in the best possible way and contributes more than he knows towards the well-being of their relationship.

Twenty-four
Through Thick and Thin
Main hoon na

Teen talk frequently falls back on a line that mildly annoys me because of its sheer banality: 'I'm here for you.' I hear it from my youngest daughter all the time. I see it on her phone and I read it in her chat room when she's furiously messaging her beloved buddies. Sometimes I ask irritatedly, 'What happened to so-and-so who used to be "there for you" last month? And where's the one who swore to be "there for you" for ever and ever?' My daughter shrugs and says, 'You won't understand, ma. Just drop it.' So I do.

Then again, I envy the ease with which these commitments are made. I invest a lot of meaning in lines like 'I'm there for you.' I take them at face value if they're uttered with sincerity by the right person, at the right time. I've grown up believing in the power of stated promises. I like to think people actually mean what they say. More fool me? I don't think so.

Couples, in particular, need to take a fresh look at their commitments and review their mission statements, if only to remind themselves of what the original vows meant when they were taken. People tend to forget. And the original promise gets lost in the mire of everyday life. But when you think of it, those teenage words 'Don't worry, I'll always be there for you' are at the very foundation of marriage, in any culture. If you can't count on your mate, no matter what, there's nothing.

A few weeks ago, as I sat writing this book, a disturbed young wife came to see me. She was feeling particularly let down and lonely at the prospect of facing yet another medical crisis on her own. Though she acknowledged it was not major, just the thought that her busy husband expected her to go through the surgical procedure by herself, made her feel unloved and abandoned.

'It's not that I can't "manage"—there's little I can't "manage" by myself. But I would have liked him to be present . . . to share my nervousness and pain . . . to reassure me I'd came out of it okay. All I wanted was for him to say, "Don't worry—I'm there." Instead, his secretary called to ask if I could handle it, or did I really want him to reschedule his meetings on that day? I felt so let down and depressed.'

Her husband isn't a villain. And I'm sure he loves her. Or, at least, is concerned about her well-being, given their young family and her responsibilities as a mother and homemaker. But the years of taking his wife and her frequent ill-health for granted have taken their toll. He doesn't feel the need to be by her side, because he feels she's more than capable of taking care of herself. This makes her sad. Very sad. She is filled with a deep feeling of rejection. 'There is no tenderness left in our marriage—just duty.'

I asked her if she felt she was responsible for his alienation. And she answered truthfully, reflectively, 'I don't believe so. I married young and was instructed to obey my husband, who is a few years older. I've done just that. Maybe that was my mistake. He told me to become entirely self-reliant since he wasn't going to be around a lot, given the amount he travels. So I taught myself to become a proficient driver, gardener, carpenter, mechanic, plumber, cook, dhobi, clerk, peon, insurance person, butler, maid, valet, nanny . . . I don't know whether or not he noticed. All I know is he could count on me to fix anything and everything around the house. I never had to turn to him for help—much as I would have liked to.'

This is the essential dichotomy of modern marriage. Women who may have preferred to stick to more traditional, less confusing roles within marriage are being forced to play a different sort of game. They want men they can lean on, men who say, 'Don't worry. Leave it all to me. Main hoon na?' Instead, they end up uttering that line themselves and feeling miserable in the bargain.

When you start looking outside your marriage for the all-important 'dependability factor', you should see it as an early warning sign that your relationship needs working on.

Reassurance. That's what every woman—and man—looks for in a committed relationship. Reassurance has such strong emotional resonance. It's a word I love saying inside my head frequently. Who doesn't need reassurance? Expecially during a crisis? The crisis could revolve around something as 'superficial' as falling hair (try telling a rapidly balding man that hair is not an issue!) to falling fortunes (try telling anyone going broke is okay!).

Marriage needs reassurance as a bedrock. We all have our anxieties and fears. We all need to know we can express them, and still be loved. A grown man can be afraid of lizards, a grown woman of the dark (I am!). People fear different things—heights, water, elevators . . . growing old, looking ugly. It is when a partner recognizes these fears, absorbs and understands them that the much-needed reassurance makes its presence felt. Check this: I need to feel reassured that I will be reassured whenever I need it!

Another wife of nearly twenty years' standing complained that she had zero jurisdiction over her residence. 'I can't really call it home, since nothing belongs to me. Nor can I make any changes on my own.' She talked about the time she had dared to move a painting from its designated position. When her husband came home, he gave the staff hell for shifting it, yelling, 'Why do you listen to her? Does she pay your salary? Don't you know who the boss is?'

She felt humiliated, to be thus put down in the presence of their teenage kids and the domestics who she spent most of the day instructing by proxy. Her husband is not a tyrant—he's just been raised to believe in his sovereignty.

'I feel like an intruder in his space,' the wife admitted, 'since I don't enjoy any real rights to carry out even minor changes. He hangs on to the keys to our locker, and also makes sure I can't operate any of the bank accounts on my own. The safe in our home is exclusively under his control, even though it contains mainly my papers, jewellery and passport. Of course I find this ridiculous, and we have talked about it. I'm an educated person. I've run my own business very successfully in the past. I find his possessiveness crazy.' And the main thing is, he is not 'there' for her when she needs him the most. Like the time she had to do double duty, when her father was ailing and her kids' exams were on. Or when his aunt was hospitalized and she was expected to take turns staying over at the hospital even though one of her own children needed her at home. The question of her husband pitching in didn't come up. Nor did he ever ask her whether she felt tired, trying to cope with all these demands.

When her own health failed, he said brusquely, 'I told you not to overdo things. You must know where to draw the line.' He didn't bother to organize medical help or take further interest, leaving her to locate a specialist, drive herself to various labs for tests, check into a clinic on her own, undergo a minor operation and, of course, pay her own bills. All this, while he went ahead with his travel and weekend leisure activities.

When she brought up the matter, he brushed off her questions saying, 'Stop nagging. You know, you have this awful habit of cribbing and complaining all the time. By the way, have you paid the car insurance? And make sure the air conditioner is serviced today—I couldn't sleep a wink last night.'

What is marriage without the all-important 'dependability' factor? Why bother to share your life, space and time with someone who's clearly on a private trip, flying solo? Many men these days insist that their wives have no time for them. And they're right. 'She has her own priorities—where do I fit in? From the time she wakes up, she concentrates on herself. She wants money, she wants the car, she wants everything on her terms. She works hard and there's a lot of pressure on her to compete. I respect her professionalism. But there's a limit. When she isn't working, she's working out! Like a maniac, at that. It's gym time or meditation and yoga classes. She has a personal trainer. A personal tarot card reader. She's into her own "wellness" trip, which excludes me completely. Her entire week is booked, packed with appointments and engagements—where's my slot? If I say that to her, she loses it and asks, "Why didn't you marry some dumb cow if that's the life you wanted? I'm not your slave to stay home all day catering to your needs!" That's so negative of her.'

So it is. Negative and short-sighted. But there are any number of ladies in the fast track who are unwilling to conform to old-world rules, even if those rules worked better in some areas of their personal lives.

Marriage, I always say, requires an enormous amount of investment. Back to my '3 T's' theory. Couples need Time, Tolerance and Tenderness to make the relationship work. These days, time has become the single most precious commodity. Most couples don't have enough of it. Most refuse to spare any for the other. Most are so possessive about time, they measure it out, Scrooge-style. As for tolerance and tenderness, God knows they're both in seriously short supply.

It's important to be able to adapt, accommodate and understand the shifting scenario. Rigidity never works, especially when it comes to emotional bonds. Both husband and wife need to define their emotional requirements from time to time, since those requirements do undergo changes, when situations alter. New-age husbands are trying to realign their thinking, but their wives are often not giving them the chance to do so in an unpressurized environment.

'We are being made to feel like villains and rogues. Accusations are flung at us constantly. Our wives blame us for everything that goes wrong in their lives. We are labelled insensitive, uncaring, selfish . . . this is bullshit, man! Give us a break, we are trying, okay? We want to be supportive— but supportive of what? Women today are just taking advantage of the situation and piling on the guilt. We men have become victims of a damaging vilification campaign.'

They have a point. I keep meeting incredibly headstrong, ruthlessly ambitious women who diminish their husbands (and themselves, in the bargain) by their aggressive posturing. To my mind, marriage demands a level of decent, decorous conduct at all times, in private as much as in public. If that's too hard, don't bother with marriage at all.

I belong to the mutual 'Main hoon na' school. I want to

be able to count on my mate in my deepest sleep. I want to have the confidence that he'll stand by me, no matter what. He may give me hell in private for something he doesn't entirely endorse, but we must present a joint front. Differences there will always be, and I consider them essential for a healthy relationship. But these should be sorted out far from public scrutiny. I want to believe that the first person I can turn to in any situation is my husband.

And he should have the same level of trust and confidence in me. These fundamentals are at the very core of any loving relationship. Without such a structure, such a foundation, there's nothing but a hollow façade that passes for marriage.

> *If complete self-sufficiency is everything, why bother with marriage at all? The decision to marry suggests a desire to share your life with another.*

Now that my two youngest children are teenagers, we spend a lot of time talking about relationships. On a recent visit to our weekend home in Pune, one of them asked about what she dubbed a 'space arrangement' between couples who prefer their own bedrooms to a shared one. Since these kids can't help but notice differences, they wanted to know whether it's 'normal' for mom and dad to live in separate rooms and lead separate lives. Parents of lots of friends whose homes they visited preferred this to being in one room.

I tried explaining how it worked better for couples facing marital hiccups to be out of each other's hair temporarily. Or how some couples preferred to have their own space (literally), especially if both happened to be in demanding careers involving frequent travel, crazy schedules and late nights on the laptop. It didn't mean they'd stopped loving each other. It meant they were confident, comfortable and secure enough in their relationship to not make this arrangement an issue. The kids didn't look convinced. 'It's weird,' they said. 'Why get married if you want to live separately?'

There's a point there. We talked about other ways of loving, sharing, caring. 'It isn't only about being in the same bedroom,' I argued. But the younger one asked a relevant question: 'What if you need something in the middle of the night? What if you feel like a cuddle or a kiss? What if you want to be hugged? Or you're scared? What if you fall ill? Or, if you have a nightmare and wake up with a fright? Do you then walk across to the other person's bedroom and knock? Doesn't it seem a little crazy? Parents should be together and sleep together—that's it.'

Most of the kids felt the same way, and suggested practical ways of dealing with demanding individual schedules. Eye shades, earplugs, workstations in a corner of the room, cellphones on silent mode. 'It's always possible to work out something that suits both, if you really want to,' said a fifteen-year-old who'd seen her own parents through a bad patch in their marriage. But all the kids were in agreement that marriage was about closeness and companionship. And that couldn't possibly get the required nurturing in compartmentalized lives.

'My father likes his books and music. My mother likes her meditation tapes and silence. But they've made adjustments to accommodate each other. I would hate to see them in different rooms,' one of them said. When I laughingly pointed out that the Queen of England and so many other royals traditionally spent the nights in their own chambers, the kids mocked, 'Look where it got them.'

As far as I am concerned, sleeping together is one of the joys of married life. Just the reassuring sight of your partner sleeping a few inches away (or cuddled up and all over you), is like enjoying a warm blanket on a cold winter night—an incomparably comforting feeling. The power of physical intimacy can never be underestimated. In fact, sex and power are subjects worthy of another book. Examine the marriages of couples you know or have observed closely. One can always tell which of the two controls the marriage sexually. It isn't about who is better looking or richer. It is about who drives the sexual equation, who pushes the sexual agenda, who presses the right buttons. Nothing rational about it. I've seen extremely aggressive men in positions of enormous power in their own fields behaving like love-sick puppies in the presence of their wives—not all of them gorgeous sex-bombs! Women who know how to make their partners happy in bed are women who end up calling the shots. It's not about cold-blooded manipulation at all.

Most women use their sexuality to advantage when faced with situations that demand it.

If a man suffers from low self-worth, and the woman somehow senses it and makes him feel like a champ in bed, you can be sure he'll love her forever and do whatever she demands. Conversely, men who make a Plain Jane feel like Bipasha Basu at her sizzling best (*Jism*, anyone?) will win her over totally.

Couples who are fortunate enough to be in sync sexually, actually glow! This may sound crazy, but it's true. Sex is the single most cementing factor in marriage, even though we'd like to believe it isn't so. Women who bring ego into their love-making generally end up in an unfulfilled relationship. As do men who behave like they're doing their wives a huge favour by bedding them.

Sexual 'dos' and 'dont's' need to be defined at the start. If a man insists on oral sex, or is keen on anal or experimental sex, if a woman likes bondage or wants her partner to go down on her—it must be stated. If you don't express your sexual needs or refuse to define parameters, you can't blame your partner for getting it wrong later.

Sometimes, I watch unlikely pairs at a party and mentally undress them. I imagine the two making love, and squirm at the image. And yet, it is so easy to tell which couples share an active, healthy sex life and which don't. It's also equally easy to tell if the woman is on top, from her body language (assertive and super-confident).

Going back to the two-bedroom theme, I have seen separate rooms working rather well in large joint families with three generations living cheek by jowl in sprawling homes. With the domestic responsibilities being handled almost exclusively by the womenfolk, it is a pragmatic way out that suits the entire extended family—senior ladies occupy their own wing, along with kids and grandkids, creating space for the young marrieds to enjoy private time in their quarters without having to deal with bawling brats and petty squabbles.

Today, it's the acute shortage of space that is leading to forced togetherness. Couples constantly complain of a lack of emotional and physical space in their cubbyholes. 'My husband often sleeps on a couch in the living room after a late-night shoot,' said a grateful wife (an ad film-maker herself). 'It's not a question of being able to snuggle up to your partner in the middle of the night, though that is important. With both of us working long and irregular hours, we need to catch up on rest. But I do miss the old days when we couldn't fall asleep without being wrapped around each other.' Now that same couple admits to experiencing a sense of suffocation. 'I feel boxed in, with too much togetherness. Especially at night, when I feel like unwinding and doing my own thing, pottering about without being forced to chat, laugh or have programmed sex.'

There it is—Main hoon na has several versions. Take your pick. It can work over long distances. And it can backfire within restricted personal space. It depends entirely on what the couple really wants—and even that is not a constant. The beauty of a relationship based on the Main hoon na principle is that no one person has to play the assigned role permanently. It works best when the roles become interchangeable, depending on the circumstances. But if either cannot satisfy the strong emotional pull of 'being there' when most needed, there's something to worry about.

For a marriage to endure, for a couple to believe in staying 'Janam janam ke saathi,' there is no single formula that is foolproof. Sex alone isn't the answer either. After all, physical attraction is just one factor, and even that doesn't remain constant. Desire fades. Desirability vanishes. Early allure gets replaced by habit and a certain staleness. Then what? Aha—then the real challenge begins.

It takes a minimum of ten years for two people to actually get to know one another. To intercept the little tricks, idiosyncrasies, quirks and accept them. Ten more to understand what it all adds up to. Who the real person you married, actually is. What living together for twenty years has taught you—about yourself and your partner. And then, another ten to finally accept your differences and come to terms with all the hiccups that might have bothered you earlier. That's when you start to appreciate one another. Enjoy sameness. And overlook the differences. It's a pretty long journey—thirty years. Are you up for it?

That is the question you must ask yourself when you embark on the road to matrimony. Not too many people are willing to wait for thirty long years to get the answer. But there is no other route. No shorter cut. Living together even for forty years is not the same thing. For that provides an instant escape route and indicates some sort of a fear of commitment.

Yes, the C-word, so dreaded by the present generation, is what counts. The way the marriage cookie crumbles depends entirely on your attitude to that one word. Don't let it scare you. After all, without your realizing it, you are already committed to something or someone—your job, parents, friends, siblings . . . so accept one more Big-C when you accept marriage. For, without it, there is nothing. Shoonya.

The Truth About Marriage

To state the obvious . . .

- ♥ There's no shame in 'needing' each other, and articulating this need.
- ♥ Sometimes, merely the sound of those soothing words 'Don't worry. Relax. I'm here . . .' makes all the difference between feeling defeated and experiencing hope.
- ♥ Dreams play a big role in bolstering morale. Don't make fun of your partner's hopes—participate and indulge. It's a far more positive option.
- ♥ Women are particularly sensitive when it comes to their health. They experience tremendous guilt as they fear burdening the family budget with medical bills. Reassurance required!
- ♥ Men need exactly the same reassurance in marriage, especially during stressful periods in their career. A wife who steadfastly stands by her partner shows not just her unconditional love and loyalty, but also the strength of her own character.
- ♥ Women must sensitize themselves to their husband's occasional and perhaps irrational-sounding demands. Just as husbands need to listen keenly, and preferably silently, to their wives' expectations.

Twenty-five
Taking Stock
Kal, aaj aur kal

It is said that couples who have been happily married for a while start resembling each other. Not only do they look alike, they also sound alike. Often, they're so much in sync, they can actually anticipate each other's thoughts and complete sentences. Some start to dress alike (sporty couples who enjoy the same game, like golf), and their body language, eating habits, accents and idiosyncrasies all begin to overlap. They almost become interchangeable! If this sounds boring to others, they themselves find it comforting, even amusing!

Synchronicity such as this evolves over a period of time,

spent in close (stifling?) proximity. Couples who achieve this unique position are generally those who are in resonance with one another at a far deeper level—the spiritual one. This is a tricky subject, since spirituality itself is so vast and so complex. But couples who do not recognize or respect the spiritual core of their partners can never achieve that wonderful level of becoming 'soul mates' that poets frequently describe, but few couples actually grow into. Cynics may mock

> *Intimacy does not grow in a cold environment. It is like a hothouse bloom. Think of intimacy as an orchid and you'll automatically nurture it.*

and say, 'What the hell, even dog owners end up looking like their beloved pets.' Very true. They do. But only if they are lucky enough to find such a pet and love the pet so deeply that they too arrive at that elusive mystical plateau where the distinction between 'you' and the 'other' gets fuzzy.

For a couple to nurture one another in the best possible way, they have to think of themselves as saplings which need light, water, sunshine, good nutrients, shelter, a pollution-free atmosphere, and enough breathing space without a giant tree blocking their growth, in order to flower gloriously. Relationships are equally delicate, especially during those crucial early years that establish the pattern for later. Shared spiritual values definitely contribute towards the state of equilibrium we all crave. I believe that when individuals respect each other in the deepest sense, they respect the cosmos, too.

My husband is a very keen student of comparative religion. He reads tomes on the subject and makes copious notes. While I'm interested and all that, my search has yet to match his level of intensity. But even though I'm not always paying close attention when he's reading out key passages from the *Mahabharata* or the Quran, somewhere something is registering.

Of late, he has taken to analyzing the *Manu Smriti*, subjecting each 'law' to such close scrutiny, I'm left totally at sea sometimes. But I greatly value the effort he makes to mark out what he thinks I should pay attention to, often taking the trouble to copy entire pages for my reference. Through his constant and patient tutoring, I have begun taking an interest in the scriptures—which I most certainly would not have done, left to myself.

I watch my husband at prayer, and I'm filled with a sudden tranquillity. It is his unshakeable faith from which I draw my strength. It is his belief, his positive thinking, that sees me through my dark days. Even though our rituals do not necessarily overlap, and my rare visits to the Kali temple in Kolkata don't leave me full of the same level of religious fervour as he experiences, I'm aware of the depth of his faith, just as he is aware of my own quirky rituals without my having to provide explanations for them.

I strongly believe a shared religion or faith acts as a powerful binding force in marriage. Even though I have several friends who have married outside their religion and are perfectly happy, I can often sense a slight embarrassment, a hesitation, when it comes to participating in each other's religious festivals and rituals. For public consumption, of course, the story they project is completely different. But in reality, the subject of cross-religious commitment does raise its ugly head.

Taking stock of your marriage from time to time is essential for an aware couple. Taking stock does not mean sitting across a table with an open book of accounts. Marriage cannot be equated to a balance sheet in which the figures have to add up. Yet, the occasional review is required, if only to look back in a positive way. Mistakes must be acknowledged and apologies issued. It is only when two people can be emotionally naked in each other's presence that one can call theirs an honest relationship. Big issues, if buried too long, tend to fester. Deal with them. Have the courage to put them on the table for discussion.

Wives often say they can't do it because their husbands don't seem to consider their big issues to be big enough, in the first place! Husbands claim their wives have got it all wrong and that women in any case tend to exaggerate matters and make them appear far bigger than they actually are. For example, men hate being dragged into 'servant problems', which seem to preoccupy women to a ridiculous extent. Husbands often crib that they're not at all interested in listening to this nonsensical 'khit-pit' ('And you know what that bitch said to me then . . .? Imagine, she was at fault, the fridge hadn't been cleaned in weeks, and when I asked why, she had the cheek to say, "Clean it yourself!"'). Women should deal with these matters themselves (or the man should, if he runs the house). Two people are really not needed for sorting out domestic trivia.

I've seen marriages collapse under the weight of constant nagging about servants, sweepers, drivers, and other domestic staff. Nobody needs to give that sort of importance to non-issues. Besides, good management principles say that a homemaker ought to be left alone to run the home without interference. If it's a collaborative effort, then separate duties must be specified. ('Okay, I'll deal with the car pool, you handle the bazaar.') Why waste time arguing over doodhwalas and dhobis? Please resolve these matters early in the marriage and let your partner get on with his or her job minus irritating advice and monitoring.

When I look back, I'm relieved to report that my husband's home was running perfectly without me, which suited everybody just fine. The routine was set and a pattern established. There was no real need for me to ruin it all by getting over-involved. Besides, to tell you the absolute truth, I'm not really bothered whether a towel or two is not back on the rack, or whether the napkin rings are perfectly polished. The kitchen is more my husband's domain than mine (he's a far better cook), and I don't care all that much if a bookshelf has not been dusted in weeks. Ours is a busy household with several children, their friends, an over-energetic dog, my visitors, our friends—I can either write or count the onions and potatoes in the pantry. You can guess my preference. Earlier on, my indifference to domestic detail used to annoy my husband. These days, he raises it once or twice a year—which is understandable. Maybe he has grown weary, or maybe our home really does run smoothly enough.

Priorities change in marriage. Nothing but nothing remains a constant, thank God. Not even nagging. Couples find new things to argue or fight about. It's fluidity which keeps a marriage alive and ticking. Today, my husband and I quibble over entirely different things—mainly our approach to 'disciplining' the two younger girls at home.

Our youngest children are still teenagers and the only time we take opposing stands is when it comes to their lives. My husband keeps talking about his teenage years and how he had to adhere to a 7 p.m. deadline. I refer to mine, when I had to stick to an 11 p.m. deadline——or else. Today's nineteen-year-old does not step out on a Saturday night before 10.30 p.m. I don't like it. I fight with the girls constantly over these absurd timings, but I know they're responsible kids who generally get home at the pre-decided time. It's hard playing policewoman. It's harder still being the go-between. But that's life today. And one has to find solutions that suit everybody.

About what tomorrow holds, who can tell? We seem to be on a good, solid wicket. May it remain that way. My girlfriends tell me I have changed beyond recognition—— 'You aren't the same human being' is the comment I hear frequently from women I've grown up with. Of course I am not! Thank God I am not! I am a married woman. I enjoy being a married woman. I cannot be the restless, sometimes reckless, often impulsive, frequently brash child-woman of the sixties. With marriage and motherhood come responsibilities and challenges. During my early twenties, I lived entirely for myself. It was a great life, but also an intensely selfish one. It was all about 'me, me, me'. Marriage changes that to 'us, us, us', whether you like it or not. There are times when I don't! I feel like yelling, 'Where

> *A healthy marriage needs the assurance that a partner will come through in an emergency, no matter what.*

am I in all this? Who is this person staring back from the bathroom mirror so earnestly? Surely not me?'

Well, it's definitely not the old me, though she is not completely dead. Occasionally, I do resurrect her, just to remind myself of the individual I once was. I'm sure my husband does the same. His life, too, was a 'rocking' one, as the kids would say, spent in Kolkata during Kolkata's glory days. For both of us, there are two distinct phases: 'pre-marriage' and 'post-marriage'. We laugh at our past and also at our present. How we've changed, we exclaim, when we look through old albums and talk about former girlfriends and boyfriends. We wonder how our lives might have been had we married any one of those contenders. Different, for sure!

Is it then, necessary . . . mandatory . . . to submerge one's personality in a relationship? Does marriage demand it? Yes and no. Marriage alters perspectives and priorities— it has to. If you resist and rebel, there's something not quite okay with the equation to start with. If you surrender and swim with your head above the water, confident that your partner won't allow you to drown, then the chances of working through your difficulties and doubts are that much higher. Some time ago, I wrote a particularly scathing article on Hillary Clinton and her selling out, when she, more than most women, could afford to have taken a principled stand. I suggested the time had come for her to assert herself and tell Bill where to get off. A girlfriend called to say she liked the column, but why was I not more vehement, more defiant? I asked, 'Honey . . . who do you want me to defy? And why?'

Defiance for the sake of defiance has zero meaning. My friend is a single woman and most of our exchanges end with the words, 'How would I know—I'm not married, thank God! I could never live by the Married People's Guide Book.' At least she's clear about that. Just as I'm clear that marriage cannot work without that Guide Book. Each couple has to write their own rules. But in the absence of a personal code, it's not such a terrible thing to follow a time-tested, universal code. Marriage cannot flourish in an anarchic, tempestuous, aggressively individualistic atmosphere. Couples can survive such phases, but at a great price.

Anne Tyler, that marvellously gifted writer (*The Accidental Tourist*) recently published a novel, *The Amateur Marriage*. I read the review ('Wedded Blahs') in *Time* magazine and was struck by one of the lines. 'We were just . . . unskilled,' Michael, the husband in the book concludes, looking back on his 'afflicted marriage'. Tyler tells us Michael hears an old song on his car radio. 'He liked the way the singer kept her voice plain and ordinary . . . too intent on expressing her sadness to concern herself with effect.' I wept, reading those poignant words. Amateur—that description says it all about

The Truth About Marriage

marriages that aren't 'ripe', for couples who aren't really ready. For all those who jump into matrimony because 'Let's get married' sounds like fun. Well, often that leads to 'Let's get un-married.' End of fun.

Follow the 'TTT' rule—Time, tolerance and tenderness. You need all three in abundance to make your marriage sing.

My younger colleagues often ask about the choices I've made, aware as they are that I have actively constructed my life around just one basic principle: Family First. They wonder whether I regret having given up this or that (a full-time, hands-on job, for example). I'd be dishonest if I said I've had absolutely no regrets—sure, I have. But those have been tiny twitches, a few pinches, really. Almost childish in their petulance. Deep down, I know I have done the right thing—for me.

I wanted marriage, I wanted family. I was smart enough (ahem!) to figure out you can't really have it all. 'Having it all' is one of those irresistible clichés that has misled a generation of gullible women the world over. Show me one woman who has it all—just one. Show me one man, for that matter, who thinks he has it all. Like all clichés that gain popular acceptance, this was the one we all fell for. How terrific it sounded. We desperately looked around for role models who would fit the bill. We tagged the line on to any woman who had achieved something even slightly out of the ordinary. We gasped at the made-for-ads images of 'superwomen' and 'power ladies'. What a lot of bilge that was and how we bought into the myth! No matter. Two decades on, we can see for ourselves how we miscalculated. Yes, we tried bloody hard to have it all. But did we succeed? Heck, no. We had quite a lot, though. More, much more than women of previous generations. But 'all'?

Women should not waste their tears looking back and moaning, 'I wish I'd done that . . . if only I'd listened to my inner voice then.' Honey, it's already too late by the time you wake up to those lost opportunities. Forget the past. Leave your yearnings for unrealized dreams behind. This is today. This is now. This is for real. And then there are all those tomorrows to think about. How you live out your life depends entirely on you. It's your future. If you feel degraded by your domestic responsibilities, do something about the quality of those responsibilities.

Often, when I wander through my favourite vegetable market, examining brinjals and cabbages, haggling with vendors of seasonal fruit, I look around and see the faces of women engaged in a similar activity. Their expressions tell me a lot about them and their marriages. Women who bring commitment into the simple act of buying onions and potatoes at the right price, bring commitment to their family life as well. Does this sound strange? Well, it isn't. A careful housewife values earnings—her own and her husband's. She knows the effort involved. And she doesn't want to fritter money away—not even on overpriced onions.

It is these fleeting, ephemeral 'subzimandi' moments that make me stop dead in my tracks and smile in recognition. I remember 'that' woman within me. And thank God she's still alive.

Sometimes, people stop to chat. 'What are you doing buying vegetables in this crowded market like any other housewife?' they ask, not bothering to hide their disbelief. I laugh at the question. What's the point of 'explaining' anything? I go back to selecting the perfect plump, purple brinjal for baingan bharta. As I imagine its shiny skin roasting, I think of my husband's distaste for the vegetable. 'Okay,' I say to myself, 'we'll cook it when he goes to Alibag.'

I stop for tea with Hasmukh, the silversmith whose shop I've been going to for over twenty years. He asks about my children, I ask about his. We discuss the stiff price charged by tuition teachers and how 'thanda' the jewellery trade has been ever since the Budget. I love these periodic chats in the vegetable market I know so well. Frankly, I can't see any other, 'rosier' picture, no matter how hard I try. Would I have had a superior life in New

York or Singapore or London? It depends on what 'superior' means.

I look back at all the choices I made (and women must make far more than men). Sure, I could have done things differently. Done them better. But I chose to opt out of the rat race early in life. I chose not to work full-time. I chose to structure my career around my home, my husband, my children. According to me, I chose well. I'm happy with my choices. That's all that matters. So many contemporaries have scaled professional peaks, travelled the world many times over, won countless awards, savoured enormous success. I feel proud of them, and happy for them. But not for a moment do I feel envious or want to switch places. Marriage was never a 'goal' for me. It was life itself, with all its crazy ups and downs, its bleak periods when I've asked myself, 'Do I need this?' and its glorious moments (surely these are what make everything worthwhile?).

I'm sure my husband has experienced something quite close to this himself—misgivings, along with mystical, magical moments, rage and romance, jealousy and compassion, empathy and alienation. Marriage is like a patchwork quilt—some patches are prettier than the others.

As I write these concluding lines, I think about the fact that today happens to be a very significant day in my life. It was on this day, many years ago, that I first I met my husband.

The Truth About Marriage

It was a day that changed both of us forever. A dramatic day in which destiny was the main star. About that, I'm entirely convinced.

There's torrential rain in the city today. It was calmer the night we met, over two decades ago. The same calm is in my heart right now. As I look across the table, my eyes rest on the dancing bamboos he has sent me to mark our 'meeting anniversary'—quite a departure from long-stemmed roses or baskets of orchids. The card accompanying the happy, healthy green bamboos is naughty. I love the contrast and the unpredictability of the gesture.

Last evening, my husband asked me what I wanted for our special day—a dinner date at my favourite restaurant? Pink champagne? A few friends at home? Something else? I waved away all his suggestions, and smiled. As I lay in bed, I asked myself truthfully, 'What do I really want from him?' I went over our early years, early fights, early patch-ups. How differently we lived our life then. How differently we live it today! If, in those days, I expected a song and dance to mark this momentous occasion, today I want nothing more than a 'normal' day filled with 'normal' activities. I feel we've gone well beyond gestures of the formal kind. It would be great to watch a DVD, maybe have a glass or two of wine, eat home-cooked food, and chill with the children. We don't really need anything more elaborate—just the comfort of home, kids, a familiar bed, a familiar body. No masks, no games, no pretence.

I flip through my 2004 diary, the fat blue one filled with pictures, notes, scribbles, letters, postcards, quotations, accounts, reminders, poems . . . oh, all kinds of things, even weekly horoscopes. And I come across a photocopy with a message to me. It is dated 4 December 2003.

It starts, 'Dearest wife—To our permanent union . . .'

Then follows a lengthy quote from the *Hindu Samskaras*, on marriage.

Marriage, a permanent and stable union. Marriage is not a temporary contract to serve the momentary physical demand or to enjoy good company for sometime and then to lapse at the slightest inconvenience. It is a permanent union which stands various vicissitudes in life only to grow stronger and more stable.

Firm and life-long companionship is the objective in view. This aspect of marriage is highly prized and the husband prays to the goddess Sarasvati, to protect it: 'Sarasvati, promote this undertaking, O gracious one, O Bountiful one, thou who will sing first of all that is; in whom what is; has been born: in whom this whole world dwells— that song I will sing today, which will be the highest glory of women.'

It is this song I want to share with the world . . . abiding and melodious, till the last and final note.

Who needs marriage?
I do.

Acknowledgements

I could have gone on writing this book for ever. It's that kind of a book—new insights every day! And had it not been for the gentle but firm (very firm!) voice of my editor Karthika, I'd still be at it.

'There has to be a cut-off point,' she said, as we sat at my dining table surveying the proofs. I was scribbling away furiously. 'Oh God! I forgot that . . .' 'Must include, must include . . . it's so important.' 'No! Don't delete this passage . . . it is key . . .'

The musical voice subtly changed tone and decibels. 'Stop!' said Karthika firmly. And I promptly did. A sensible author never argues with a good editor.

It was time for a late lunch. And some fun. Chapter

headings are generally such a bore to write. Why not familiar Hindi film songs or film titles? I suggested. Why not? Karthika agreed . . . and began humming. Before we knew it, we had slipped into nostalgia, remembering old, forgotten melodies, popular movies, cheesy lyrics. Chapter headings? A mere excuse for a lusty singalong.

If only all editors were as gifted!

I owe three other ladies a huge debt. My mother, the 'nameless' one. Born Shakuntala, renamed Indira after marriage, but addressed as 'A-ga' (impossible to translate!) by my father all through their time together (a few months short of sixty years, when she passed away). There is much I learned from this extraordinary lady, who had instinctively figured out the truth about marriage, and lived by it throughout her life.

Indumati Vrajlal Kilachand was my mother-in-law for ten years. From her, I learned another of life's most valuable lessons—timing. Timing may not be everything, but it helps when you live in a large, extended family, with three generations and several sensitive egos. The trick is to shut up when you have to, and speak only when you need to. Induben, as everyone calls her, is eighty-eight years old now, and as shrewd, wise and observant as she was when we first met. An exemplary wife, she was her husband Vrajlal's most trusted counsellor and companion, through great times and tough times, till his death in 2003. She has always known how to manage her family, her finances, her responsibilities and traumas. But mainly, she knew how to 'manage' her husband in the best possible way—with love and respect at all times.

And finally, a small tribute to Poornima, my husband Dilip's mother. I never did get to know her, for she passed away years before I married her son. Strangely, I can sense her presence in our lives. Sometimes, while writing, I look at her framed portrait, less than two feet away from where I sit, and I want to thank her for giving me the person I share my life with.

To these women, my gratitude. To wives of the world, my encouragement. To husbands, a warning. As they say in India, 'Mind it.' A successful marriage relies heavily on the subtle art of negotiation. Flatly stated: women make better negotiators!